CYCLES
and
RENEWAL

WILLIAM M. RAMSAY

CYCLES
and
RENEWAL

Trends in Protestant Lay Education

ABINGDON PRESS Nashville and New York

CYCLES AND RENEWAL

Copyright © 1969 by Abingdon Press

Library of Congress Catalog Card Number: 69–12023

Scripture quotations unless otherwise noted are from the
Revised Standard Version of the Bible, copyrighted 1946
and 1952 by the Division of Christian Education, National Council of Churches, and are used by permission.

SET UP, PRINTED, AND BOUND BY THE
PARTHENON PRESS, AT NASHVILLE,
TENNESSEE, UNITED STATES OF AMERICA

To DeVere, My Wife

ACKNOWLEDGMENTS

For what values there are in this book, thanks are due to many.

It was the Board of Christian Education of the Presbyterian Church in the United States and its staff which made possible the study leave during which I did the research reported here. Special mention must be made of Dr. Marshall C. Dendy, then executive secretary of that board, Dr. William Bean Kennedy, and Dr. Harmon B. Ramsey, who encouraged me in taking the study leave. My wonderfully capable colleagues, the Rev. Arthur M. Field, Jr., Miss Estelle Rountree, and Miss Patricia Mills, did my work for me, as well as their own, while I was away studying.

Three professors taught me courses especially useful during this study and read and criticized early versions of the manuscript: Dr. Alan Knox, Teachers College, Columbia University; Dr. C. Ellis Nelson, Union Theological Seminary, New York; and Dr. George W. Webber, also of Union Theological Seminary. Prof. Richard T. Murray of Perkins School of Theology at Southern Methodist University and the Rev. A. S. Tippit of the National Council of Churches also made helpful suggestions.

And most especially thanks must go to the staff members of many denominations and of the National Council of Churches, to leaders of independent lay movements, and to ministers and members in many local churches who shared with me accounts of the remarkable work they are doing in adult education.

CONTENTS

INTRODUCTION

"You will meet a band of prophets coming down from the high place with harp, tambourine, flute, and lyre before them, prophesying."

"God may or may not be dead," a Roman Catholic editor joked in an article in the *Saturday Review,* "but the new Christianity is a swinging thing." [1] The article, entitled "The End of 'Black Book' Publishing," discussed the changes in Roman Catholic publishing policies but could have described almost equally well the ferment in Protestant religious education.

This book is about some of these changes as they affect Protestant adults.

On a given Sunday a visitor to the right places might quite likely chance upon:

a group of young adults drinking in a church-sponsored coffee house while they listen to a bearded folk singer and his guitar;

an elderly lawyer lecturing to an even more elderly group of women on the prophecies of Malachi;

a group of college students at an independent "renewal" center vehemently denouncing the suburban church because it is unconcerned about race, war, and poverty;

a businessman/teacher in the men's Bible class of a suburban church vehemently denouncing the church because its educational program is "meddling" in such matters as race, war, and poverty;

a little group of mixed ages sitting around a table, slick paperbacks before them, earnestly debating subjects relating to race, war, or poverty;

in a hundred thousand living rooms, ankle deep in the Sunday paper, hundreds of thousands of men and women, church members or pagans alike, unaware of or simply uninterested in the whole business, idly flicking on their TV's to watch a church-produced program such as "Look Up and Live."

Indeed, as the churches prepared to enter the final quarter of the century, there were dozens of other forms of Protestant adult education.

There was perhaps not a significant program of adult religious education in any denomination which some other group of equally committed Protestants did not denounce. But for all the often lamented "marginality" of adult education in the churches few Protestant thinkers denied its importance. The traditional ladies' Bible class had a determined loyalty which was not to be disregarded. The Pentecostal Full Gospel Businessmen's Fellowship saw desperate need for their preparations for the last days. The avant-garde theologians preached prophetically of the necessity of "training the laity for mission in the world."

A critic once charged that the Protestant Sunday school is an organized confusion. This is as true of Protestant adult education as of any other part of the church's educational ministry. It would take a larger and more scholarly book than this one fully to explain all that is going on in the bewildering and constantly moving picture which represents contemporary lay study programs. But this volume is intended to be useful for heroic but puzzled teachers and the members of their classes, for hurried and frustrated pastors who find a strange discrepancy between the ideal they read about in their denominational manuals and the reality they see in their congregations, for parish committees who plan for adult study, and for my fellow professionals in Christian education. This book may serve as a kind of primer for them, a brief and partial introduction to what is going on, to what has gone on, and even to what may someday be going on in the fascinatingly revolving realm of continuing education for church members.

This book makes no claim to completeness. The adult education effort is far too widespread and varied for one short volume to achieve a fully balanced survey. It makes only a limited claim to objectivity. I have tried to be objective in my account of various programs; but I am a staff member of a denominational board of Christian education, and, inevitably, not only my reasoned judgments but my prejudices may show. Let the reader be warned thus in advance to beware of them.

This book does propose to try to help the reader understand better what is going on in the adult education program of his church by helping him to look at it from certain particular perspectives.

First, there is "the renewal movement." Deliberately designed to shake the church out of old established patterns, the movement has sought to bring what our grandparents would have called a "revival" and what in secular circles would be called "revolution." Chapter I will explore something of the challenge the renewal prophets are hurling at the ecclesiastical establishment.

Second, there is the curious history of lay education in the church with its cycles of ups and downs, of lay leadership and professional leadership, and of structure and independence. Whether it stands rigidly in the pattern of tradition or has revolted determinedly against it, every study group is influenced by that history. Chapter II will tell something of this story, especially as it relates to American churches in this century.

Third, there is the most widespread phenomenon of the past decade in the education of the mainline, "established" Protestant denominations, the new curricula of the 1960's. The Episcopalians, the Baptists, the Methodists, the Presbyterians, the United Church of Christ, the Lutherans, the Disciples—indeed, almost every denomination to which readers of this volume may belong—produced by the thousands new study materials for adults within these ten years. Chapter III is intended to help the reader understand where the new study program of his church came from and what effect its carefully planned cycles and spectrums are intended to have on him and his denomination.

How some established churches in the traditional denominations have broken with old patterns and ventured out in new and independent ways in response to the renewal challenge is the subject of Chapter IV.

Chapter V, based on this analysis, gives my own predictions and proposals for Protestant education in the years that still lie ahead. The proposals may be of use to the reader as he considers the future of his own church's study.

1

THE
RENEWAL
MOVEMENT

"Do not be conformed . . . but be transformed by the renewal of your mind."

Some churches professed to be finding new life in the new curricula the denominational staffs were producing. John R. Fry, formerly of the United Presbyterian Board of Christian Education, had a different notion as to what to do about his sometime colleagues: fire them! "The denomination could maintain an allegiance to the poor by actually giving them money, and could open dozens of hospitals a year with the savings on airline travel that would be gained by firing the staff." [1] The professionals' first concern, he charged, was to protect their own institutions. Mass dismissal of the greater part of them would be, he felt, good riddance.

Appropriately, Fry's charges first appeared in *Renewal Magazine,* for challenges to the ecclesiastical establishment were an essential part of the 1960's "renewal movement." It did not really matter that the salary figures Fry quoted were actually double those with which a staff member was likely to begin or that Fry seemed a bit naïve about the actual cost of opening a new hospital these days. The point was that the renewal movement's leaders felt the prophetic call to challenge the old ways. And many of them, like Fry himself, were heroically at work in the inner city practicing all that they preached.

Actually Fry's proposal of firing the administrators was relatively mild. Some renewal enthusiasts turned their attention to the churches themselves. *All* the existing structures were seen as under judgment. Gordon Cosby, whose Church of the Saviour, in Washington, D. C., had inspired many both in and out of the movement, was on record by the mid-60's as concluding that

the present institutional structures of the Church must give place to new structures that will *be* the Church on mission. This conviction has come to me gradually—I have worked with it consciously for the past fifteen years and have been disturbed about it for the past three. Now I am convinced that the institutional structures that we know are not renewable.[2]

Specifically Cosby proposed openness to such possi-

bilities as the giving up of all professional ministries
so that every pastor would earn his own living in
some secular way. Giving up all real estate by the
church, all church buildings, seemed to Cosby worth
considering too. Nothing need be left but little bands
of people "on mission."

Joseph Mathews of the Ecumenical Institute in
Chicago and Howard Moody of the Judson Memorial
Church in New York were ready, instead, to celebrate
"the end of religion." "Toward a Religionless
Church for a Secular World" [3] was the title of one of
Moody's articles, and by Advent, 1966, Moody,
though still obviously a Christian, was preaching on
the end of all "ideologies"—including the Christian.

In the next chapter we will review very briefly
something of the history of Protestant adult education in America. That summary will show that what
is probably going on at your own church is in part
what the renewal leaders have been protesting. It will
also suggest the honorable ancestry of the renewal
movement. Chapter III will describe the curricula
of most denominations, suggesting that they are both
a cause and a result of the renewal protests.

But for any man who wants to understand the new
things happening in his church classroom, there is no
better point of beginning than a look at some of the
famous modern renewal efforts.

One note of caution: the term "renewal movement" is here used to cover the work of a multitude
of prophets. It has no clearly defined limits. Some
parts may be thought of as relatively moderate in
approach. Robert Raines, for example, is often in-

cluded among the renewalists though he is pastor of what in some ways seems a typical suburban church. Others, we have noted, are much more extreme in their approaches. By 1966 a bibliography on the movement had already been compiled containing some 2,000 titles. All that can be attempted in this chapter is one observer's brief survey of some of the aspects of the movement which seem most relevant to Protestant adult education.

Broadly, it was clear that in the minds of leaders of the renewal movement a renewed church would be a missionary church. But mission was defined not so much in terms of an evangelism which would aim at fitting men for the next world as of service to mankind in this world. The church, William Temple had earlier pointed out, exists in behalf of those who will never darken the door of the church. A "renewed" church would follow a Savior who had taken the form of a servant. Its saints would be equipped for the work of ministry, of service. It would be the body of and would share in the mission of the Christ who came concerned for the poor, the liberty of captives, and freedom for the oppressed. It must be concerned not simply to serve its own members but the world. It would be a church for others, a church turned inside out.

To many the American churches seemed ingrown and dedicated to the preservation of their own institutions. Against that kind of established Christianity the renewalists revolted.

Origins in Europe

Appropriately, the origins of the attack on American organization of the churches are to be found in Europe, where the typical American activist bureaucracies had never existed.

In the days following World War II, Europe had discovered to its surprise that it was now a pagan continent. Abbé Godin shocked Europe with his question: *France a Missionary Land?* [4] Most Frenchmen, it is true, were baptized, married, and buried at the church. Thus they attended three times, though they had to be carried in twice. Only 10 percent were found to be regular at Mass. Similar situations were observed in nearly every other European nation. In Western Europe, Christendom had ended.

In 1948 the World Council of Churches was born, and soon it was addressing itself indirectly to this problem. Hans Hoekendijk, a Dutchman and former missionary in Southeast Asia, was made head of a department of evangelism. Hoekendijk was to advocate radically changed structures and approaches for reaching a radically changed world, turning "the church inside out."

In Germany evangelical academies sprang into existence, designed to promote dialogue between church and world. The exact relationship of these academies to the churches, however, was not always clear. Often the academies received little sympathy from the established congregations, and they did not always manifest great sympathy in return. Their groupings were not those of a particular parish. Rather, the

21

typical academy might bring to its retreat center a cross-section of personnel from some industry, both management and labor, or a group made up entirely of people from one profession, such as physicians or teachers. Moreover, the discussions centered around not simply the Bible and Christian doctrine but the work in the world—including its politics and business —in which these adults were engaged.

The movement took other forms in other countries. In 1950 I found myself as a theological student at Iona in Scotland mowing the grass on the tombs of long-dead Scottish kings while discussing theology with a Greek Orthodox priest, an English boy studying to be an actor, and a Scottish gardener. In 1957 as a typical American visitor at the Scottish "Kirk Week at Aberdeen" I found myself quite at home with the well-organized conference format but startled by the subject matter under discussion. For though I had been to many such conferences in the United States, at all of them we had talked about what we do in the church: teaching Sunday school, the work of world missions, how to run a men's group, etc. Here, with equally clear Christian devotion, the Scots were discussing what it means to be a Christian in the office of a shipyard or as the headmaster of a small school.

New theological approaches were being developed, too. The World Council itself was both a product and producer of a new emphasis on the ecumenical church. Seminary courses in systematics, which had once concentrated on such dogmas as Christology and creation, expanded their discussions of doctrines about the church. And with the studies of the church came studies of the church's mission. The word "evangelism" was given new life. Evangelism acquired new meaning, too, with a strong accent on witness by deeds rather than by words.

Studies sponsored by the World Council and books on evangelism from abroad began in the 50's to make their impact felt in America. George Macleod of Iona, both in person and through his works and through those who had visited the island, became known. D. T. Niles's *That They May Have Life* [5] was widely studied. Tom Allen wrote *The Face of My Parish*.[6]

Perhaps the book most directly influencing adult education in this country was *A Theology of the Laity,* by the World Council's Hendrik Kraemer (1959).[7] The very words of the book were to be quoted over and over as catchphrases in all sorts of materials dealing with adult education, from bureaucratic memoranda to renewal prophecies: "the church is mission" (never "has a mission") ; "the ministry of the laity" (never "the work of church members") ; "training" (never "educating") "the laity" (never "adults") "for mission" (never "missions") "in the world" (never "in the church"). Kraemer had laid down a platform for adult education for the ecumenical church.

Morphology and Americans

The 1960's, however, found the church still unrenewed and the mission not yet accomplished in the world. The World Council, assembled at New Delhi,

India, in 1961, believed that it had discovered at least one part of the reason. The church itself was not organized for mission in the world. Indeed, it was centered around a residential parish system which had been developed for villages in the Middle Ages and which seemed rather to insulate the church from the areas of business and politics where the real decisions were being made. "The Missionary Structure of the Congregation" became a six-year study theme for the World Council. In each area, including North America, a study group was appointed to explore the whole question. The sickness of the church began to be diagnosed as, in part at least, "morphological fundamentalism," a rigid adherence to old organizations— including old educational organizations—in a new world.

It is interesting to note that the North American working group for this study was to reflect considerably the influence of four subgroups. One group were the people from other countries. Thomas Wieser, a Swiss, served as secretary and wrote up the findings of the group. Colin W. Williams, an Australian who had come to the staff of the National Council of Churches, was influential. Jitsuo Morikawa contributed from his Oriental heritage. And Hans Hoekendijk, imported from Holland to teach at Union Theological Seminary in New York, arrived in time to make his mark. It is especially interesting to note the influence of these men from outside the United States, since this nation's own problems were so different from those of Europe. There the church seemed to be dying. Here the postwar church had experienced a phenomenal boom. If some wondered that the North American report should be considerably the work of those not from North America, others felt that this gave it a much needed perspective.

Another group sharing in the report were from unusual structures which had come into being here. George W. Webber, who had left the East Harlem Parish for the Metropolitan Urban Service Training program, Letty Russell of the East Harlem Parish, and William H. Hollister, pastor of Christ Church, Presbyterian, housed in a Burlington, Vermont, TV repair shop, made contributions. To their work we will return later.

Third, there were theologians such as Harvey Cox and Gibson Winter. These two, and others such as Peter Berger, had been writing books which without using the term "adult education" (not generally in the approved vocabulary of the renewal movement) obviously had bearing on that subject. Each was knowledgeable in the field of sociology, Berger thinking of himself as a sociologist rather than a theologian. In such books as *The Noise of Solemn Assemblies*[8] Berger had blasted away at the religious establishment. Here in America he saw no need for a world/church dialogue because we have, he felt, only a secularized church in a pseudo-Christian world. Gibson Winter had decried what he called *The Suburban Captivity of the Churches*.[9] The congregation centered in a residential area simply could not be relevant to the inner city, the world of work, and the political decisions which so increasingly dominated life. Harvey Cox pled with the church to take a fresh look at *The Secular City* of 1965,[10] seeing urbanization not as a threat but as a gift of God. The secular world, he argued, need not be brought into the church to be authentic. The church was not to be a "religious service station" but rather was to aid people in becoming authentically human. Perhaps the church need not even mention the word "God" for the next few years, Cox suggested. Most churches, however, continued to do so.

Finally, there were representatives of various denominational boards. Relatively few pastors of "successful" suburban churches were on the committee.

"One basic conflict we faced," George Webber recalls, "was determining exactly what our job was. Some felt our task was to decide what new structures might be the best ways into which to reshape the existing residential congregation. The more radical group felt we should forget about all existing structures, start from scratch, and take a fresh look, asking not how to patch up the old, but just what kind of structures are really needed in our day. These might perhaps not be residential parishes at all."

To some, at least, it appeared that the more revolutionary-minded group won.

In 1967 the findings of the North American committee were published under the title, *The Church for Others*.[11]

The Effect in Christian Education Literature

Though as noted above, renewal enthusiasts did not as a rule say much about either Christian education or adult education, they did urge "training the laity for mission in the world." "The older programs of adult education ran the danger of a kind of 'incest,' " Dr. Webber warned. "The term 'lay training' stands for an effort to get us out of our self-contained educational box. It presupposes some basic Christian understanding and commitment. 'Lay training' seeks to help Christians now to develop the skills necessary for authentic witness in today's world." However valid the distinction, many Christian educators were quick to notice the significance of the renewal discoveries for their concern.

One contribution made to the literature of adult education was the accounts of the new lay training centers. Professor Lee Gable described those of Germany in *Church and World Encounter*.[12] Donald G. Bloesch wrote in 1964 of *Centers of Christian Renewal*[13] in this country and abroad.

Robert Raines attributed *New Life in the Church*[14] in part to little *koinonia* groups throughout his congregation.

Two of the "renewal churches" had gifted writers to spread their gospel. George Webber's inspiring account of *God's Colony in Man's World*[15] described the East Harlem Parish. And his *The Congregation in Mission*[16] included an account of his use of small discussion groups and how the sermon was related to the study in the East Harlem program. Elizabeth O'Connor, secretary of the Church of the Saviour, Washington, D. C., described the two-year-long training program required for membership there.[17] Significantly, she reported that the small discussion groups which had been so vital in the early days of the church had become ingrown. They had sprung to life again, however, as they were transformed into mission groups, centering not on study but on action.

Appropriate to the electronic age, Christ Church, Presbyterian, in Burlington, Vermont, became known best through a kinescope of a TV program discussing its concentration on small mission groups.

The new training centers produced periodicals and newsletters, too. The Detroit Industrial Mission, the Ecumenical Institute in Chicago, the Faith and Life Community, and many others thus spread their message of creative and novel approaches. *Renewal Magazine,* then published by the Chicago City Missionary Society, had produced by 1966 enough outstanding articles for them to be collected under a title which suggested their iconoclastic stance, *Who's Killing the Church?* Each periodical professed to be not only about lay training but also for laymen themselves to read.

Perhaps in the category of renewal literature one might list two rather negative books directly related to adult education. Bruce Reinhart's *The Institutional Nature of Adult Christian Education*[18] analyzed with the care of a trained sociologist the programs of adult education in nine Bay Area churches, found them often prostituted to the interests of the survival of their insecure institutions. John R. Fry's *A Hard Look at Adult Christian Education*[19] sought to appeal through denunciations rather than research.

Small mixed study groups, for example, were interpreted in language with Freudian connotations. Why, Fry demanded, did couples in such groups never discuss with each other their sex acts? Was it not because they really were brought together by sex? If sex was a factor, this seemed somehow evil to Fry. He did not discuss whether he would prefer sexually segregated groupings. Fry's chief positive proposal was that adults might better their education by reading good books.

The World Council's structures study produced its own reports. More directly related to Christian education was the book by the Rev. Letty Russell of the East Harlem Parish, *Christian Education in Mission*,[20] published in 1967. Though she concentrated on the education of children and youth as it was carried on in her own Church of the Ascension, certain implications obviously were related to adults, too. Worship was tied to study in meaningful ways; the church's nature as a family was emphasized; and the place of task forces and structures of continuing presence in areas of special need were described. Clearly not only inner-city but suburban churches would profit from her writing.

Finally, from the literary standpoint the renewal movement was making its contribution through study of its books in established churches, where they were frequently used as texts. We shall note in Chapter IV how many adults in more conventional churches were studying such volumes as *The Secular City* and Trueblood's *The Company of the Committed*.[21]

29

New Wineskins

The real impact of the various renewal programs, however, lay not in a bunch of books. The establishment could publish books. Rather it lay in the experiments themselves—and in the experimenters. One could argue with this or that aspect of George Webber's theology, but no one could argue with his tireless devotion to mission work in the slums. One might be put off by the purple prose of the publicity releases of the Ecumenical Institute, but it was hard not to be impressed by the communal living of its staff.

It would not be possible to describe in one volume all the new, more or less independent and nondenominational institutions which had appeared by the mid-60's for the purpose of pioneering in the renewal of the church. The following brief account of three of these ventures is intended to suggest some things characteristic of many of the others.

1. Basically the most controversial of these three was the Ecumenical Institute, an affiliate of the Church Federation of Greater Chicago.

Time magazine called it a "laboratory for the future" of Christianity. In glowing words the institute advertised its purpose as being "to articulate the mood, style, and pattern of the post-modern world-view and to enable individuals in all areas of life to formulate their own self-understanding for the sake of significant involvement in civilization." Within this intent was the "concern to advance the civilizationing process, to promote human dignity, and to develop an attitude of globality." Courses were supposed to appeal to "vanward students," "lucid individuals today," and "sentinel adults." Actually, in a recent year 16,000 people were sufficiently vanward, lucid, and sentinel to crowd into its cramped, slumbound facilities for at least a two-day session. What they got there was often a crash course in such thinkers as twentieth-century theologians Tillich and Bonhoeffer. The surprisingly young faculty taught eagerly with what some observers called "the shock treatment." Staff members from the Institute were sometimes available to lead similar conferences in locations throughout the nation

"Boy! They really know their sociology!" a Baptist educator exclaimed admiringly as he described for me how the Institute had analyzed for his group the life of Chicago and the needs of its inner city. Indeed, emphasis at the Institute was so strongly on life in this world that some adherents tended to deny the reality of any next world at all. One of their publications rejoiced in "the end of religion," which it suggested was then—in the mid-60's—at hand. But the families of its youthful staff not only shared with each other in common worship and common meals; they identified, in Christlike commitment, with the poor of the ghetto in which they had deliberately chosen to make their home.

2. Representing perhaps a relatively conservative approach to renewal outside usual church structures was the Laymen's Movement. In sharp contrast to the Ecumenical Institute, which chose to be stimulatingly controversial, the Laymen's Movement as a matter of

policy avoided taking any official stands on the subjects of social concern which its members might discuss at their meetings. Instead, "we emphasize
prayer," I heard one executive of the movement explain: "private, corporate, and in small groups."

The movement's avowed aim was "to help each
member develop the inner resources he needs to live
his deepest convictions and contribute meaningfully
to the lives of those around him. It seeks to help members find the power of God in their own lives." Emphasis was placed on the practical benefits of "faith
in God, in man, in yourself." Publicity of the movement spoke of "a new experiment in successful living."

A major means for achieving this obviously worthy
purpose was its retreat center at Wainwright House,
Rye, New York. Here programs might include study
conferences, "quiet days," and seminars on spiritual
healing.

But the movement spread its ideas nationwide by
encouraging the formation of "personal groups,"
which typically took the form of businessmen's break-
fasts or luncheons for worship and study across denominational lines. The group helped institute the
interdenominational observance of Layman's Sunday
and the establishment of the meditation room at the
United Nations Building in New York.

3. Occupying a mediating position among renewal
efforts, the Yokefellow movement had as its purpose
"commitment in depth for the renewal of the
church." D. Elton Trueblood, Quaker philosopher
and prolific author, served as president and charis-

matic leader of Yokefellow Associates. Conferences of various kinds, often on weekends, were provided for ministers and laymen at the Yokefellow Institute at Richmond, Indiana, near the Earlham School of Religion, an institution of Quaker background but with an ecumenical faculty. Such varied leaders as Roger Shinn and Joseph Fletcher might be on the retreat staff for different weekends in the same summer.

The influence of the movement radiated in the 60's far beyond the conferences at the center, however, due in part to the wide popularity of Trueblood both as a lecturer and a writer. Small groups of "Yokefellows," organized in churches of many different denominations and across denominational lines, also spread the new approach. Yokefellows, who sometimes wore small gold pins representing the yoke of Christ, accepted a six-point discipline which included daily prayer, scripture reading, proportionate giving of money, and systematic study. The movement emphasized the fellowship of small, disciplined groups and stressed ministry in the world, in vocations, and in the structures of society, such as government, industry, and labor.

"We aren't an organization; we're a movement," board member Robert A. Cox, a dentist of Cambridge City, Indiana, told me. "And we are an ill-disciplined disciplined group," he laughed. "That is, nobody tries to check up on you. You sign your discipline card privately. It's up to you and God." Indeed, I found that many who attended the Yokefellow Conference in 1968 were a little puzzled when I asked, "Are you a Yokefellow?" "We don't keep any membership rolls," Dr. Cox explained. "We are only a loose fellowship. We don't want to start a new denomination. But we are all committed to working within the existing structures and sometimes in small groups for the renewal of the church."

Yokefellows in the western states, it is true, had become incorporated. They published study materials, including recordings, which placed emphasis on self-understanding through relationship within groups. The retreat center at Earlham, on the other hand, perhaps placed more emphasis on action for peace and justice in society. But Trueblood appeared to be making in the late 60's a strong effort to manifest the underlying unity of various renewal efforts. He pled with Yokefellows to have *both* "roots and fruits," inner discipline *and* social involvement. For the Yokefellows' fifteenth-anniversary convention laymen braved blizzards to come from Minneapolis and Florida and Dallas and Rochester. There they heard representatives from such diverse groups as the Laymen's Movement, the Church of the Saviour, Faith at Work, LAOS, and International Christian Leadership explain their different approaches for their common goal, the renewal of the church.[22]

Renewal Congregations

There were congregations, too, which were equally determined to burst out of traditional patterns. Several of these had become as famous as the independent centers.

1. The East Harlem Parish, for example, had

found ways of worship designed to express the gospel and our response to it in terms most meaningful to a disadvantaged community. An adult study group during the week might explore with the minister the passage to be the basis of the sermon the next Sunday. Some members would share in teaching it to the children in Sunday school. The sermon would then take on deeper meaning. At the Communion service at the Church of the Ascension I found myself exchanging "the kiss of peace"—modern style, by shaking hands—with nearly every member present. The Maundy Thursday Communion included an *agape* meal (of sardines, bread, and cheese) and "foot washing"—again modern style, by brushing off shoes. The Tenebrae service concluded with the extinguishing of candles in a darkened church so that the people would go out, like Judas, into the blackness of night to await Good Friday. Through such worship one "learned" at a level deeper than the intellect.[23]

2. Turn the church into a theater! This seemed, at first glance at least, to be part of the answer of Judson Memorial Church, a congregation having ties with the American Baptists and The United Church of Christ, located next to New York University in the heart of Greenwich Village. The large auditorium had been transformed into a rough theater, with great floodlights mounted from the choir loft and homemade dressing rooms partly blocking the light from the stained-glass windows from another era. One might find on Sunday morning the entire chancel area filled with garish hand-painted scenery from a

play to be given there that evening. For that matter the morning service one Sunday in Lent, 1967, was devoted largely to a play for children. One Lenten service substituted for the sermon a song and dance performance in praise of freedom. The 1967 Easter service included a beautiful ballet to a musical setting of words from the Song of Songs. When at the climax of the service bearded percussionists in their hippie garb beat a roll on drums and struck a huge Chinese gong during the singing of "Christ the Lord Is Risen Today," one felt the whole congregation was sharing in joyful celebration of the good news.

Even more impressive was "the sharing of concerns," which preceded the morning prayer, for the matters about which prayer was requested seemed usually to be not so much individual wishes as expressions of social responsibility: for peace in Vietnam, for civil rights, or for local political action. "The reason we're leaving our church in New Jersey to join Judson," one couple told me, "is because this church really seems involved in what is going on in the world." "Sometimes the most important part of the worship is the announcements," Howard Moody, the Judson pastor, commented. "They show what the church is really concerned about." [24]

3. What made the Church of the Saviour in Washington, D. C., sufficiently newsworthy for a feature article in the *Reader's Digest* was in part its adult education program. Other churches, of course, had something comparable to its School of Christian Living. What made this one unique was that two years of serious study in it were required before one could be

admitted to membership in the Church of the Saviour. Regular attendance was expected at the weekly hour-and-a-half sessions, with written assignments required. The courses themselves were on rather traditional subject matter: Bible, doctrine, growth, ethics, stewardship, etc. The classes, however, appeared to put unusual emphasis on personal encounter. Their church secretary reports:

What is important in any School of Christian Living is that we present the unmistakable implications of deep and total commitment involved in following Christ— the challenge and risk and danger, the promise and the cost. The content will always be unimportant alongside the experience of Christ himself.[25]

When the applicant for membership had completed the required courses, he could enter continuing elective classes. For membership he was also expected to prepare a paper stating "what Christ means to me," what spiritual discipline he was undertaking, what areas in his life seemed to be in most need of help, and what specific work he was doing through the church and how long he had been engaged in it. Each member, new or old, was given into the care of a "spiritual director" for continued prayer and counsel and was likely soon to serve as "spiritual director" for another.

I asked the pastor, Gordon Cosby, what was the key to the success of the Church of the Saviour's School for Christian Living. "There are many things, of course," he told me, "but if you want just one, it's the assignments. Class members are required to experiment outside of class with what they have learned. For example, if we are studying the inner life, the student is expected to try certain devotional exercises during the week to find out how hard it is to meditate and perhaps to report on his experience. Or if we are studying Jesus' commandment to love, a class member may be asked to pick three people for special practice during the week: a friend, someone he doesn't like, and a 'neutral' person. He may be asked to discuss or write up his findings growing out of his experience of trying to manifest love in these specific situations. And of course these assignments must be carried out. Auditors are admitted to our courses only by special permission of the instructor."

4. Christ Church, Presbyterian, Burlington, Vermont, buried both weekly worship and Sunday school in order to emphasize that Christianity is best expressed in service.

Ten years after the church was begun, the little congregation still met in a former TV repair shop, a reminder that a church is not a building. Involved almost from the beginning in work at a coffee house, the city jail, and the Lund Home, the church had centered much of its life around the task groups working in these places. But in the proposal of June 6, 1966, members read:

Yet, in spite of thoughtful pronouncements and "outrigger" mission activities such as The Loft, Lund Home and jail groups, Christ Church continues to center its life and functions around the Sunday morning exercises of church school and worship, and the Sunday evening period of study.

Our Sunday gatherings are thought of as "home base," or the axle of a wheel, and the church's mission groups are thought of as the spokes that extend into and move through the world.

This notion is wrong. The church exists only for God's mission in the world, and mission must therefore *be* the "home base." Every action of the church should center on the places in the world where we are called to serve as God's agents of peace, justice and reconciliation. And so let us now, once and for all, abandon the Sunday "home base" heresy. . . .

The Loft, Lund Home, Jail, Occupational and other mission groups *are* Christ Church, Presbyterian. We have only to grant them the freedom (time, for example) to authentically carry out the liturgical functions of service, worship and study.[26]

To this end the church completely abandoned the typical weekly program of Sunday worship and church school. Study, worship, and fellowship would be concentrated instead each week in the little groups of members on mission in the world.

True, Christ Church members were expected to participate in an all-day "monthly festival" once a month. Their program for the festival in November, 1966, for example, involved an hour and a half of study of assigned chapters in John, led by the pastor, youth studying with adults, and further study of the same chapters with all ages working together in art projects, drama, and poetry or dance centered around the scripture theme. After lunch, strategy discussion included reports from the various groups. (Recreation and naptime facilities were provided for the children.) The weekly meetings of the task groups at the jail or the Lund Home involved study of the same passage.

Adult education thus remained essential to the process. But Christ Church made it clear that education was not *the* essential. Mission was the essential. They would take no chance on study that might never get around to "applying the lesson to life." That, they were sure, was to get the order all backward. They would begin with service. When men were involved, study was sure to follow.

Challenge to the Churches

"What did you mean," I asked Gordon Cosby, "when you said of the church 'the institutional structures that we know are not renewable'?"

"I meant just this," he replied. "The church exists to do two things, and it isn't really set up now to do either one of them. First, there is 'the journey inward.' We are to help people see themselves, to confront their own sin and the radical claims of Christ upon them. And second, there is 'the journey outward' to be on mission in the world today. If that's not the purpose of the church, then I don't know what it is for. But with its thousand-year-old pattern of organization the church can't really do either one of these things. We just aren't set up either for the nurture of deep devotional life or to channel radical obedience into the world. We are set up to serve ourselves—and that often in superficial ways—not to serve mankind."

"Then what would you do if you were a layman, say in the insurance business, and were a member of an established church, say First Church, back home?"

"I would try to gather a small group who meant business. We would try to work together on both the inward and the outward journey, the devotional life and service in the world. We would probably get into trouble, though. People would say we were trying to be holier-than-thou, that we were a self-righteous clique. I would carry on in the church as long as I could. But they might put us out."

"What would you do," I asked Howard Moody of Judson Memorial, "if the Lord called you from Greenwich Village back to your native Texas to be, for example, pastor of the First Baptist Church of Dallas?"

"I couldn't possibly say," he smiled, "any more than I knew what I was going to do when I came here. Every church has got to work out its own program indigenous to its own situation. The program at Judson has evolved as the church and the community have changed. We don't claim to have a pattern for anybody to imitate. That's been tried two or three times. It bombed."

Perhaps it was not the function of such churches and of the independent centers to propose new programs or patterns for a new establishment. They were not out to give universal answers. But they were asking universal questions. How can men and women be helped to look at the world as Christians? How can the church move out of old ruts into channels of grace? What is the right relationship between study and worship and action? How can education get deeper than the top of the head? In what forms and by what methods can adults best face the twentieth century as followers of Christ?

Sometimes as he looked at the response of the established, traditional churches to his challenge, the renewal prophet felt himself to be but a voice crying in the wilderness. Yet, though they were all too few, in cities and in suburbs, one could find echoes of their call to prepare. Established churches and denominational bureaucracies did, here and there, seek the road to renewal. In fact, they had sought it often in the past, and revolt against the established clergy-led order was not a new thing in the training of adults.

An account of some past experiments in lay education is the subject of the next chapter. The tradition to be described both created the establishment against which the renewalists revolted and—in certain ways, perhaps—created the revolt itself. The reader may find his own history described there, too.

2

SOME CYCLES
IN THE HISTORY
OF LAY EDUCATION

*"And you shall remember all the way which the
Lord your God has led you."*

"We used to go to church," commented one of the
characters in the comic strip "Peanuts" one morning
in the late 60's, "but now we go to a coffee house!"
Most Christians, however, in spite of all the new
forms of the renewal movement, still worshiped and
learned in traditional congregations. Chapter IV will
return to the renewal movement and the impact it
was having on the established churches. This chapter,
however, will review something of the establishment
in adult education and how it got established.

Within Protestantism protest against tradition was itself a part of the tradition. The renewal movement has had an honorable ancestry, as have the conventional forms against which it has rebelled. The laymen breaking out of old patterns to establish mission-oriented groups unsanctioned by the clergy have had their forerunners. So have the harassed professionals seeking to develop training for laymen who sometimes did not want to be trained. The themes of activism *vs.* intellectualism, independence *vs.* structure, liberalism *vs.* conservatism, and lay movement *vs.* bureaucracy have appeared before, and doubtless will again. If "education for mission" was the renewal slogan of the 60's, it was not entirely different from some goals of the 1920's.

I once heard theologian-educator Sara Little reacting to a lecture by a religious educator whose views have recently become popular. He had pled for a higher place for the insights of psychology in curriculum planning in a manner suggestive of the progressive educators of the 1930's, had voiced a theology in which she detected echoes of Schleiermacher and nineteenth-century liberalism, and had advocated an experience-centered approach to religious education not unlike that of George Albert Coe of the 1920's. "I know we are 'post-Barthian,'" Dr. Little commented to those about her. "But I can't help feeling we've been here before. I know *we've been here before!*"

The intention of this chapter is to help the reader understand what is going on in his church by looking at it from a neglected perspective. It is the perspective afforded by a brief and highly selective history of adult education in the churches in America, especially in this century. Perhaps as he looks at the cycles of history, he too may feel that "we have been here before" and thus form some ideas about where, for better or for worse, we of the church are going.

The Nineteenth Century: Independent Lay Movements

A case might be made that through much of church history, lay education has been forced to be a do-it-yourself effort. Therein has lain both strength and weakness.

Robert Raikes, founder of the Sunday school movement, was a layman. The teachers whom he hired for the first Sunday school were laymen too. In 1780 Raikes paid them a shilling a day to teach the urchins of Gloucester the catechism and literacy. The Sunday school as it grew up in the United States carried into the twentieth century something of the character of a "people's church," lay-directed, with lay-conducted worship services and lessons which were often lay sermons, in contrast to "church," which was the province of clergy. Not all clergymen were happy with the new program. Indeed, many a church in the early 1800's split over the controversial new idea of having Sunday schools. Neither the original Sunday school, however, nor most Sunday schools of the nineteenth century included classes for adults. Protestant adult education activities found their origins not only in the Sunday school movement but also in other programs.

Benjamin Franklin, with his American mixture of puritanism and pragmatism, symbolizes one strain in the lay education tradition. In him the idea of self-education is personified. He founded in Philadelphia the Junto, designed as a study and discussion group for young men which would enable them to teach each other "history, morality, poetry, mechanics, or other parts of knowledge." Among the questions to be discussed were not only such "worldly" matters as how a man might recently have made a fortune but also such "religious" subjects as the happy effects of virtue and ways of service to mankind.

More direct ancestry for modern adult religious education, however, can be traced to a Connecticut farmer and his interest in "natural philosophy." In 1826 Josiah Holbrook originated a series of meetings for cooperative study which he called the Lyceum. By 1835 there were three thousand Lyceums scattered over the new nation. The Lyceum was to bring to its platforms not only showmen like P. T. Barnum but such ministers as Ralph Waldo Emerson and Henry Ward Beecher.

Laymen developed the YMCA with its educational activities beginning in 1851 in America. Lay-led and mission-minded, it emphasized both Bible study and broader educational concerns.

Even more important, it was a layman, Lewis Miller, who teamed with a Methodist minister, John H. Vincent, to establish the Chautauqua program in

1874. Originally Chautauqua was designed for the religious education of laymen who taught Sunday school. It was to give rise to many similar programs all over the country.

An early enthusiast of the Chautauqua circuit described it in the following terms:

It is a great summer school, lasting from one week to six weeks, sometimes even longer, but usually two weeks. It is usually located in a beautiful spot near a body of water, with quiet woody places all around. Along the shores of the lake are tents and cottages where live the regular patrons. Upon the hill is a summer hotel for transient visitors. All around are tennis courts and golf links. In the center is the great auditorium with its seating capacity for thousands. . . . Picture a community in a place like this, a community gathered with the common purpose of combining mental stimulation with physical recreation. They begin each day with religious worship. . . . They repair to their classrooms, their lecture halls, their studies . . . later to hear some great man or woman statesman, educator, clergyman, or reformer discuss a topic of the day.[1]

Modern Methodists who know Lake Junaluska, Baptists who love Ridgecrest or Green Lake, or Presbyterians who each summer visit Montreat or Ghost Ranch will recognize that the Chautauqua pattern has continued into the present. Indeed, in the late 1960's the original Lake Chautauqua was drawing such varied speakers as Bryant Kirkland of the Fifth Avenue Presbyterian Church of New York and Colin Williams, then of the National Council of Churches.

1900-1920: Beginning the Big Bible Class Era

The modern adult education program in Protestantism may be thought of as beginning with the Baraca Bible Class of the First Baptist Church of Syracuse, New York, in 1890. The movement spread so rapidly that by 1905 there were five hundred Baraca classes in New York state alone. The original class was designed for young men. Baraca means "blessed" or "happy," and the class's announced aim was "to make happy every young man who comes within our circle." The pattern of the class was to close each session with a "five-minute handshake." The movement produced organizational manuals, emphasized attendance at temperance rallies, urged its members to attend worship services, sponsored baseball leagues, and sometimes may have tended to submerge its educational concerns in a sea of other religious activities both social and evangelistic.

Philathea—for "lovers of God"—Bible classes for young women began spreading in 1898. Though both movements crested in the early 1900's, many similar classes and groups of classes now appeared throughout the United States. A large congregation was likely to have many such classes competing with each other for attendance awards.

Thus the "established" pattern of adult Christian education in the first decades of the twentieth century was one of sexually segregated classes of adults, each as large as it could get to be; each to a considerable extent independent of local and denominational ecclesiastical structures; each an heir of the revivalistic evangelical theology and ethos of the Sunday school movement of frontier days and of Dwight L. Moody and the early YMCA and Chautauqua movements; and each—in some places at least—pretty much in competition with the others even within its own congregation. The Uniform Lessons provided the uniform curriculum.

Toward the end of the 1960's many could remember such classes from the Sunday schools of their own childhood. Many readers of this book can look at their own Sunday schools and find similar groups still active today.

1920-40: The Era of Institutionalism

The American Sunday School Union—later International Sunday School Union—began in 1824 outside the control of the denominational organizations. The International Union Lessons, the overwhelmingly favored curriculum of adult Bible classes, were to a considerable extent the result of efforts led by a Baptist layman and a Methodist minister to lead the Union's convention of 1872 in this direction.

By 1910, however, the denominational bureaucracies organized the Sunday School Council of Evangelical Denominations, a group they could control. The next twelve years saw the two organizations competing with each other. The denominational executives won. The merger of the two in 1922 produced what was soon known as the International Council of Religious Education (ICRE). In 1929 the Methodist Episcopal Church, South, called M. Leo Rippy to direct its program of adult education, probably the first denominational executive of this kind. The following year the ICRE employed the Rev. Harry C. Munro, a Disciples minister of somewhat liberal orientation, to be its director of adult education. The era of institutionalism had begun.

Harry Munro proved to be a leader both progressive and aggressive. Under his leadership adult Protestant education began a period which saw a bureaucracy of more or less expert denominational leaders in Christian education attempting to pour the new wine of contemporary theological and educational insights into the old wineskins of the adult Bible classes. At least three types of "new wine" may be noted.

1. Progressive education had by the 1930's gone a long way toward transforming the public schools. Educators sought to begin with the pupil where he was, to meet his individual needs through programs building on his particular interests, and to involve the learner actively in the process. A pupil-centered approach was advocated in opposition to a content-centered plan. New methods were developed.

2. Among church leaders of the 20's and 30's liberal theology was developing. The new movement was as interested, perhaps, in the saving of society as in the saving of souls. Not the transmission of information about the Bible "plan of salvation" but the development of Christlike concern for the needy became its emphasis.

A merger of these two lines of thought, expressed by such teachers as George Albert Coe, lay behind the Graded Curriculum, which reached approximately its present form in the 1920's. But the Graded Curriculum was for children and youth. In the era of child-centered psychology no graded curriculum for adults was ever developed.

3. The mushrooming of the adult education movement provided the third ingredient for the new Protestant ventures. According to a rough estimate by Malcolm S. Knowles, total enrollment in adult education activities rose from about 15 million in 1924 to about 22 million in 1934. Edward Lee Thorndike's *Adult Learning,* showing dramatically that adults can be educated, was published in 1928, just as Rippy and Munro were beginning their work. General adult education was developing its own bureaucracies, with the Department of Adult Education of the National Education Association being formed in 1924 and the American Association of Adult Education in 1926. Adult education was developing its own theory, methodology, and institutions, and it was making its importance clear.

Harry Munro was at home with each of these three movements. He was actively associated with the hierarchy of secular adult education. Theologically, though he was a trinitarian, he was a liberal who rejected any "education of imposition, fixing its attention upon passing on a ready-made holy book or body of revealed truth, or sacred institution, or set of behavior patterns." [2] It was Munro who gave dynamic leadership to the effort to transform adult education throughout Protestantism.

In his important, though at this writing unpublished, 1965 doctoral dissertation at the University of

Chicago, Dr. Kenneth Stokes has described Munro's efforts to introduce the new theology and methodology into adult education.[3] Munro seems to have attempted a three-pronged stimulus for Protestant learning. If one prong did prove blunt and bent, the other two turned out to be quite effective.

1. The effort to instigate a new mass lay movement (the first prong) was not permanently successful. The United Christian Adult Movement was born at the Lake Geneva Conference in 1936, with Harry Munro as its chief executive. The depression was beginning to wane. The war clouds did not yet hang heavy. A liberal optimistic theology was still ascendant. Secular adult education was booming. The UCAM was to be not an organization but a mass lay movement, as the Sunday school movement and the adult Bible class movements had been before it. It was hailed as a landmark in a new effort for "the building of a new world in which dwelleth righteousness." "The development of the kingdom of God" was one among its objectives. Somehow the UCAM never developed the kingdom. As a mass lay movement it hardly developed at all. Practically, the movement was allowed quietly to expire in a world in which dwelled not righteousness but World War II. This was the age, not of lay movements, but of ecclesiastical organizations. The functions of the UCAM were gradually absorbed by the International Council of Religious Education.

2. Munro's second type of approach was to continue effective for a much longer period. At first under the auspices of the UCAM, Munro and his allies helped plan a notable series of conferences on

adult education which continued, except during the war, every year or two until 1964. Such conferences introduced denominational leaders to new methods, to the findings of the newly developing social sciences, to the thoughts of outstanding theologians, and to the special ministries required for work with families, young adults, and older adults. Probably the chief reason for the decline and ultimate demise of the series was that by the 60's the various denominations had acquired staffs of their own, now trained to the point that they were capable of putting on equally effective programs for their own constituencies.

3. Munro's third approach was with pen and printing press. Here again he was effective. His committee attempted a revolution in the content of what adults would study, seeking to move away from the limited biblicism of the Uniform Lessons. They began with a curriculum guide published in 1934 and the subsequent distinguished series of editions of *Learning for Life*. This booklet, whose very title indicates its rootage in the progressive education movement, listed eighty different courses—later often called "electives" —with a choice of textbooks, from which the adult class could select its program of study. Indeed, *Learning for Life* looks very much like the manuals on flexible programs of adult education one may still get from his denominational headquarters thirty-five years later!

Booklets of the late 30's and the early 40's dealt with a new approach called "group process," with the newly discovered "young adults," and with home and family education. By 1950 a quarter of a million such pamphlets had been sold. If good pamphlets could have transformed the Bible class, the 40's would have brought a revolution of renewal.

Many classes did change. But as late as 1964 Dr. Stokes found denominational leaders reporting that the Uniform Lessons were still more popular than electives. Somehow, not everyone got all the message of the little booklets.

Part of the problem, of course, was that World War II shriveled the denominational staffs and aborted the progress.

The denominational boards burgeoned with the end of the war, however. And some of the returning servicemen became powerful new local allies for the denominational leaders who sought to bring new life into the adult Bible class. Richard E. Lentz, who now occupied the position Munro had held, wrote *Making the Adult Class Vital*,[4] and thousands of adults seemed ready to try. The new young couples did not feel at home in the large "women's Bible class" or the "old men's Bible class." They wanted to be together. And new subjects and new methods appealed to them. The International Council of Religious Education—which in 1950 merged into the National Council of Churches—sponsored conferences on young adult work. Soon many churches had formed new and rapidly growing classes for young adults. The religious boom was beginning. Clearly it was not simply age which attracted the couples following World War II. These classes tended to stay together long after the members became mature adults. By the late 50's it was not uncommon to find "young adult classes" in many churches which included on their rolls men and women in their 40's and, sometimes, new grandparents. Lively methods and new subjects of study drew and held these people. Well-equipped classrooms for adults began to replace the Akron-plan assembly halls. Harry Munro's dreams seemed to be coming true.

1940-60: The Professors Join the Professionals

In the first third of the twentieth century, as we have seen, adult education in Protestant churches had something of the character of a mass movement among laymen. By the end of the second third it had become increasingly institutionalized, with each denomination employing professionals who sought to remold the program in fashions which they believed to be better balanced and more effective. The second third of the century also saw an increasing body of theory developed about the education of adults.

The professors began to enter the picture as early as the 30's with scholars like Earl F. Zeigler and Lewis J. Sherrill writing on adult Christian educaation.[5] Much of the wisdom of the later how-to-do-it books can be found anticipated in their volumes. It was in the 40's, however, that the theologians really began to influence the denominational boards. That story has been well told elsewhere and will be only summarized here.[6] But three interrelated movements must be mentioned.

1. Neo-orthodoxy, imported and domestic, supplanted the liberalism of the 20's and 30's. When Prof. Harrison Elliott asked in the title of his 1940

book *Can Religious Education Be Christian?* [7] Prof. Shelton Smith replied, in effect, "No! Not, at least, on the old basis of John Dewey's substitution of democracy for Christianity and growth for conversion." [8] The evangelical voice of Karl Barth began to be heard in the boards. Harry Munro protested the new theology as "a retreat into authoritarianism." But words like "revelation" and "sin" began to replace words like "growth" and "adjustment" in the vocabulary of the professionals.

2. Closely related, the new biblical theology of the time taught Christian educators to speak of the "Word" and "the one story" and even the *kerygma* (the proclamation of the gospel). Professor James D. Smart, known not so much as a student of education as of theology and Bible, was brought to Philadelphia to lead in developing the Presbyterians' new Faith and Life Curriculum.[9] "People have said we were Barthians," Dr. Smart told me. "We weren't necessarily that. But we were trinitarians. And we were determined that the program of Christian education should take seriously the Bible and the doctrines of the church." The Bible was to "ask its own questions" rather than being used "to answer our questions about life."

3. The ecumenical movement within Protestantism burst into new life with the close of World War II. As the United Nations was being born, so the World Council of Churches appeared (1948). With it came a new interest in and understanding of the church, with a rediscovery of Christian education as the

church's program of teaching.[10] "Sunday" school was dead. "Church" school was the approved phrase.

Meanwhile, back at the universities, general adult education was developing into a sophisticated field of graduate study. Two great and again closely related movements were to be especially important to adult education in the churches. Both had to do with what psychotherapist Harry Stack Sullivan was to call "interpersonal relations."

Counseling began to assume a new importance in the secular world and soon within the church. Seward Hiltner baptized the client-centered or nondirective counseling theories of Carl Rogers, and seminaries began to use his books as texts for their new courses. The alliance between client-centered counseling and pupil-centered teaching had been made clear in one of Rogers' own books.[11]

The most important development of the time for the literature dealing with the psychology of adult education, whether within or outside the church, was the exploration of group dynamics. Kurt Lewin had taught the nation that the way to lead boys' clubs was not by autocratic or *laissez faire* approaches but by democratic leadership. He had demonstrated that the way to persuade housewives to buy organ meats (heart, liver, kidneys, etc.) during the meat shortage of World War II was not through persuasive lectures to large audiences but through small group discussions. The principle was applied far beyond food marketing. Human relations training laboratories began to appear. A new jargon developed. "Teacher" and "class" were out. "Leader" and "study group" were in. "Perception," "brainstorming," "feedback," and "change" became as familiar terms in the 50's as had been "growth" and "experience" in the 30's.

Synthesis for the Religious Education of Adults

It became the task of thinkers of the 50's to relate these new and diverse movements—and others not here discussed—to the task of the religious education of the Protestant laity. The task was accomplished with what appeared to be considerable success.

It was Prof. Sara Little, among others, who pioneered in popularizing in ecclesiastical circles the discoveries of group dynamics study. Her *Learning Together in the Christian Fellowship*[12] remains a highly useful summary for the lay teacher of the practical methods growing out of this approach. Robert S. Clemmons, of the Methodist board, added his *Dynamics of Christian Adult Education*.[13] Group dynamics studies resulted in both books and programs. At the University of Indiana, Paul E. Bergevin and John McKinley not only wrote *Design for Adult Education in the Church*[14] but also instituted training in "the Indiana Plan." Study groups following the program spent regular periods reflecting back on their own group processes as well as studying texts. Students at Indiana interested in church adult education work began to take not only short-term courses in the field but graduate degrees. Indeed, in the late 60's throughout the country more doctorates in adult education had been awarded to professionals in religion than to educators in any other field except agriculture.

Reuel Howe and Paul Maves brought the new insights of psychology to church practitioners of adult education through *The Creative Years*[15] and *Understanding Ourselves as Adults*.[16]

Not all the newly recovered concern for small groups came, however, from professors of psychology or counseling. By 1957, thirty-five hundred Episcopal clergy and directors of Christian education had been trained in two-week laboratories of the "Church and Group Life" program. In 1956 the National Council of Churches conducted its first Protestant laboratory in group development, a program which has continued each year until the present. Many denominations began similar programs.

Moreover, there were reports from the grass roots that group work was successful! John Casteel's *Spiritual Renewal Through Personal Groups*[17] was a kind of series of success stories from churches where cell groups had proved effective. "Why haven't we been told about this kind of religion before?" Casteel's report quoted a Utica layman as exclaiming. Protestant adult educators undertook to tell everybody the great gospel of the small group.

Attacking the subject of adult education from the other side, Robert E. Koenig related the new developments of biblical scholarship to lay study in *The Use of the Bible with Adults*.[18] Helen Khoobyar's *Facing Adult Problems in Christian Education*[19] used theological insights to relate education to life's questions.

Perhaps the outstanding book on adult education by any single author, however, was *A Philosophy of*

Adult Christian Education, by David J. Ernsberger.[20]
Dedicated to the memory of Lewis J. Sherrill, the
book was a popularization of research done by Ernsberger at Union Theological Seminary in New York.
In it Ernsberger succeeded in weaving together the
biblical and theological developments of the time
with a balanced approach to small-group work, beam-
ing the whole at the parish minister.

If Ernsberger's was the outstanding volume of a
single theory-builder, the Workshop on the Christian
Education of Adults at the University of Pittsburgh
in June, 1958, was the outstanding single scholarly
event. Under the leadership of Prof. Lawrence C.
Little there were brought to the same platform theologians like Daniel Day Williams, specialists in adult
education like Malcolm S. Knowles, sociologists such
as Thomas R. Bennett, professors of Christian education such as C. Ellis Nelson, and staff people such as
Gerald E. Knoff. Little edited the papers and address
under the title *The Future Course of Christian Adult
Education.*[21] A second Pittsburgh conference in 1961
focused on what was indeed to be the "future course,"
the preparation of the huge programs of the 60's, the
new denominational adult curricula.[22]

There were beginning to be, as we have seen,
prophets of renewal who were ready to denounce all
that the new programs were attempting. There was
good reason to believe that neither lay movements,
denominational establishments, nor professors had yet
done more than make a dent in mass Protestant religious illiteracy and introversion. But Protestantism

entered the 60's determined, in denomination after denomination, to use all available resources, lay, professional, and professorial, to create what the Methodist slogan was to call "A New Curriculum for a New Day."

3

THE
NEW
CURRICULA

"Of making many books there is no end."

Four years in advance, the United Presbyterians had the details computed. Their estimates indicated that in 1970 their new curriculum would require *283 carloads* of paper. A new curriculum is a major undertaking.

Pioneers in the process, the Presbyterians had launched their earlier Christian Faith and Life Curriculum some twenty years before. They had been forced to mortgage the Witherspoon Building in downtown Philadelphia to do it. The General Assembly of the Presbyterian Church, U. S. (the Southern

Presbyterians) authorized the borrowing of a million dollars to finance their Covenant Life Curriculum. Other curricula have been rumored to have cost as much as two or three millions.

"I won't be around, of course, if we ever start another curriculum," one denominational chief executive in Christian education once sighed to me privately, "but if anybody wants any advice, I'll be glad to tell him a few things *not* to do!" The labor in planning was enormous. Promoting was tremendous. Leadership training just to introduce the new United Presbyterian curriculum was scheduled to involve some twelve hundred specially prepared trainers. "We would have liked to do more with adults when we launched our Seabury Curriculum in 1955," said Richard Johns of the Protestant Episcopal Board of Parish Education. "But, frankly, with the curriculum for children and youth we simply didn't have the resources to do all we wanted for adults."

Neither the Episcopalians nor any other denomination planned to slight adults in the new curricula that appeared in the 1960's. Perhaps no other movement so characterized religious education of the decade as the production of new study materials for adults. Any understanding of how the mass of Protestant laity who are involved in Christian education are being trained must include a look at these programs. Almost certainly, the denomination to which you belong has attempted one of these new curricula within this past decade, and there are adults in your church now involved in its study. A brief account of several of these curricula will be found in the appendix of this volume.

A Brief Review of the Background

In 1948 the United Presbyterians launched their Christian Faith and Life Curriculum. Thousands of their classes of adults began discussing their new magazine *Crossroads*. At first the International Uniform Lessons had a place in *Crossroads*. Soon the magazine was devoted entirely to new-style lessons and articles, relating to theology, Bible study, and ethics, all written with a concern for serious study. Many pages sought to communicate in fresh ways to modern man. "The Layman's Theological Library," a series of attractive little hardback books designed for individual reading or for discussion by adult classes, was published during the 50's by the Presbyterians' Westminster Press.

The Episcopalians, as noted above, did not seek to involve adults in their Seabury Series in quite the way that they enlisted children and youth. But they did produce sober-looking hardback tomes which might be used for this purpose and which were especially recommended for church school teachers. These were marketed in the 50's under the solemn general title "The Church's Teaching."

It was perhaps the "Faith for Life" series, interdenominationally sponsored through the Cooperative Publication Association and aimed especially at younger adults, which really set the pattern of small flashy-looking paperbacks as systematically planned competitors for the older lesson quarterlies. By the time these appeared in the late 50's most of the denominations were beginning long-range plans for the curricula they were to launch in the next decade.

One reason for the new approach was frank disappointment with the results of the old. The International Uniform Lesson Series, still the staple of most adult classes, had long been out of favor with the professionals, for reasons to be noted below. Electives, such as those listed in *Learning for Life,* had not proved as successful an alternative as had been hoped. By the end of the 50's adult enrollment in church schools had already begun a slight decline, though the population of the nation was continuing to grow. Though electives gave adults—at least theoretically— a chance to study what they wanted to study, this was little help with adults who didn't seem to want to study anything. The trend in secular education was away from the elective idea, too, as "progressive education" began to mature into other patterns. Lawrence Little's survey quoted one teacher as describing a situation denominational planners feared was too typical. There were, she complained, "fifteen different Sunday schools" in her church, meaning fifteen uncoordinated adult classes.

There was one weakness in that. After the Sunday school continued for many years, people got in the habit of always going to the same class, and the class usually kept teaching the same materials. Some of them chose Bible study. One class accepted a strict literal interpretation of the Bible. Another class studied the Bible based on Roy Smith's booklets, a much more liberal interpreta-

tion. Sometimes you wondered if it was the same Bible
when you went to two classes on alternate Sundays. . . .
The thing wasn't organized. . . . There was no planned
curriculum.[1]

Curriculum planners by the late 1950's were already aware, in part at least, of what the surveys of
the 60's were to reveal about how little adults were
actually learning. For example, a survey conducted
by the ethically concerned United Church of Christ
in 1966 was to report that only about half its members
included in the survey agreed to the proposition that
"the Negro is right in demanding his full civil rights
now," in spite of the prophetic stand that denomination had repeatedly taken on civil rights. More than
half felt that "Negroes are trying to move too fast
to obtain justice and equality." And feelings among
its members were likely to become strongly negative
where integrated housing seemed a threat.[2]

According to another major denomination, in 1966,
26 percent of their class members believed that Acts
was an eyewitness account of Jesus' ministry.[3] Only
5 percent of their adult class members thought they
could quote the Ten Commandments; 18 percent
identified Leviticus as an Old Testament prophet;
42 percent had not looked at their lesson materials for
a month.

The United Presbyterians are officially heirs of the
theology of John Calvin. Their survey in the mid
60's, however, revealed that 42 percent of their laity
seemed to regard salvation as a reward for ethically
legal behavior, while only some 15 percent really
regarded it as a free gift of God's grace.[4]

It would be wrong to trace the genesis of the new curricula to a sense of discouragement by Protestant educators. Scientific surveys of this kind are still too new to give comparative figures. It is not certain that adults would have done better on the various tests given them had these been administered in the 20's or 30's. Clearly, however, there was in Protestant education room for improvement.

And there were developments that brought hope that such improvement could be achieved. Reform was permeating secular education. The missile that launched the Russian Sputnik had launched an agonizing reappraisal of American schools. By 1955 general adult education programs in their various forms had reached an estimated total enrollment of 50 million, involving perhaps 25 million different adults (most were enrolled in more than one program). The young adult movement, growing up after World War II, had shaken many a Sunday school out of old patterns with adults.

The publicity materials which introduced the new curricula seldom mentioned the surveys. Rather, they presented the new materials with slogans that combined something of Madison Avenue with something of the evangelist's call. Typical is this passage from Methodist promotional materials designed to introduce their curriculum for adults, 1967 model, Adult Studies for a New Day:

Something new is going on in God's world—something fantastic, and relentless, and a little frightening. The

Lord is moving in our common human history in a way that is both exhilarating and threatening. We hardly know what to make of it. We hardly have words to point it out, much less define it. Yet here it is . . . and here . . . and here! All over the globe the church is learning to respond to this new work of His.

The Methodist introductory materials emphasized not only the changing world but also changing church concepts of ministry, mission, and service in that world. "Inward" ministries were described as ways of empowering people for "outward" ministries. And to that end Methodists, various varieties of Presbyterians, Baptists, and Lutherans, the United Church of Christ, the Brethren, the Disciples, the Church of God, the Reformed Church in America, and other groups, separately or in cooperation, within the one decade of the 1960's undertook to provide the adults of their respective denominations with new curricula for "a new day."

A Theological Look at the Books

Death-of-God theologian William Hamilton joked about the efforts of curriculum builders to present theological developments to the common man. A transcript of part of the tape of his lecture at the University of Chicago Law School in May, 1966, reads as follows:

"The Protestant Churches have been very resourceful in recent years in taking rather striking and exciting phrases in the theological world and reducing them to triviality. 'God active in history' has had this done to it; a whole curriculum has been built upon it by denominational executives, based on this phrase which has a lovely history. 'God's will is secularization' is now being given this same treatment: [It is] a perfectly appropriate phrase in certain contexts which has now become part of the ideology for certain movements—in the inner city ministry, for example. The administration of the Protestant establishment has this capacity of taking lively and resourceful phrases and saying of them, 'Well, we believed them all along!' But what about the death of God?—we can't do it with that one!"

Dr. Hamilton might have been startled to learn that the United Presbyterians the next year had put out a pilot issue of their new curriculum journal *Trends* centered around a single theme, the God-is-dead discussions. Though always lagging somewhat behind the latest developments in biblical and theological study, the builders of the new curricula did make a serious effort to help lay people wrestle with current theological issues. Perhaps they did so with more integrity than Hamilton's quip implied.

Perhaps the most striking thing about the new curricula for adults was that they were all very much alike. Tear off the covers, and it would be quite difficult to tell which materials were Lutheran or Presbyterian or United Church of Christ.

The similarity became embarrassingly clear at a meeting of the National Council of Churches' Commission on Adult Work in 1964. Each member had been encouraged to bring some new book which would be of interest to the other adult educators.

The representative of the Lutheran Church in America proudly brought the first volume for adults in their new curriculum, a study book surveying the Bible from Genesis to Revelation and entitled *The Mighty Acts of God*. The representatives of the Presbyterian Church, U.S. brought the volume for one year of the Covenant Life Curriculum "spicle" (spiraling cycle), also surveying the Scriptures from Genesis to Revelation and, by curious coincidence, also entitled *The Mighty Acts of God*. The representatives of the United Church of Canada placed beside it on the display table *their* new adult Bible survey book, bearing exactly the same title, *The Mighty Acts of God*.[5] Each of the three appeared to be referring to the same Deity.

The Mighty Acts triplets illustrate one common characteristic of the Protestant curricula of the 60's; they were all Bible centered. It is true that in most denominations the new curricula were subject to cries from fundamentalists that "there's not enough Bible in it!" Few such complaints, however, came from adults who had actually attempted the Bible study the new books called for. Any layman who really attempted *all* the study suggestions proposed by Prof. Arnold B. Rhodes in the Covenant Life Curriculum's version of *The Mighty Acts* would be matching a seminary student in searching the Scriptures.

Repeatedly the new materials affirmed that the Bible is authoritative, normative, and unique. The placing of the Bible study books first in the sequence of most curricula was symbolic of the importance attached to the Word.

Most curriculum planners had attended seminary in the days when the theology of Barth and Brunner was making its strong impact on American thought. One may detect reflections of this in such passages as the Cooperative Curriculum Project's statement about the Scriptures: "The Bible is unique, . . . the normative source of the church's message, . . . the library of revelation, . . . not only a record of how God has revealed himself in the past. . . . It is also a present instrument of revelation." [6]

To fundamentalists schooled on the Uniform Lessons the new curricula did bring some shocks. The various *Mighty Acts* and similar volumes represented a reaction against the fragmentation of scripture, an accent on the "one story" of the whole Bible. Subsequent courses in each curriculum studied individual books of the Bible as wholes. More threatening was the approach represented by the following statement from a teacher's guide on ethics published by the Lutheran Church in America: "The study materials in this course have been deliberately structured to prevent a literalistic, mechanical application of texts to situations. To use a literalistic application is both to misuse the Bible and to block thoughtful consideration." [7] Biblical materials were plentiful in this course and in others and were often brought in quite directly. But the method was not always traditional.

By the standards of the Bible departments of many Protestant theological seminaries the critical stance of the curricula of the 60's was conservative. The multiple authorship of Genesis and of some of the prophetic books was discussed quite frankly, and there was no effort to shield the layman from the problems of relating the creation story to the theory of evolution. The documentary origin of the Gospels was described. But Bultmann's demythologization proposals had not yet in the late 60's been adopted by most of the popular paperbacks from the denominational publishers; and while there were many references to the *kerygma,* few thoroughgoing form critics were asked to write lesson materials for Protestant church schools. It may be noted that few voices were yet raised in protest within the mainline Protestant establishment about this omission.

There was a similar agreement among the curricula as to theology, with a rather conservative but by no means fundamentalist stance adopted by nearly all. C. Ellis Nelson often reminds his classes in Christian education at Union Theological Seminary in New York that if you want to see what the working theology of a denomination really is, you should look at its curriculum. This may tell more about its beliefs today than would a study of its historic creeds. If so, Protestantism had become somewhat theologically homogenized by the mid-1960's.

Perhaps it was in statements of goals that the theology of Protestant adult education was clearest. The slightly global statement of objective of the interdenominational Cooperative Curriculum Project had marked similarity to that of most of the denominations.

The objective for Christian education is that all persons be aware of God through his self-disclosure, especially his redeeming love as revealed in Jesus Christ, and that they respond in faith and love—to the end that they may know who they are and what their human situation means, grow as sons of God in every relationship, fulfill their common discipleship in the world, and abide in the Christian hope.[8]

As with the general plan of the Cooperative Curriculum Project, so with its statement of goal: there seemed to be something in it for everybody.

At least one of the major curricula did have a distinctive approach to objectives. The United Presbyterians had rejected the Cooperative Curriculum's all-encompassing statement in favor of a five-point program outlined in terms of behavioral skills. Their curriculum, in which the United Church of Christ was sharing, was designed to help its students develop five abilities needed by Christian adults: (1) to be able to interpret the Bible; (2) to explain the beliefs of the church and participate in its life; (3) to work for church unity; (4) to live as committed Christians; and (5) to deal with ethical issues and work toward solution of ethical problems.

At the same time that the curricula of the 60's were being produced, the church bookstores—as we saw in chapter I—were being flooded with books of the genre often called "the literature of renewal." In 1959 layman Hendrik Kraemer had proclaimed that "a theology of the laity," properly understood, would call for training the laity for mission in the world, that mission being understood in terms of ministry; that is, service. The so-called secular meaning of the gospel, subsequent writers were to affirm, could be understood only as a religionless Christianity was proclaimed to a secular world through service. The far more radical "death-of-God" theologians were able to dispense with the Deity himself, but Jesus-like ministry in this world was still their prime concern.

The curricula of the 60's would not convey this message to the mass of Protestant laity. The renewal slogans, "education for mission," "ministry in the world," and "let the world write the agenda," could be found in abundance scattered through the literature of Protestant adult Christian education. But they were always in a context of other concerns. Either the curriculum planners had not yet fully grasped the renewal message or they regarded it as too narrow, as one truth among several. Most were ready to affirm the service concern, but as one part of a balanced goal.

I mentioned to Gideon Wick, director of adult education for the Lutheran Church in America, that we had discussed their curriculum for an hour and a half without his once uttering any of the catchphrases of the "training-the-laity-for-mission" type. He agreed, but reminded me of the strong ethical concern of their curriculum. In our conversation United Presbyterian Edward Trefz was quick to say that "the worldly situation sets the agenda for study." But the curriculum objectives listed above, while clearly reflecting a place for the concerns of this world, obviously are also designed to help prepare people for the next. "We don't mean that anything goes," Mr. Trefz explained. "We aren't trying to indoctrinate people to take 'a Presbyterian stand.' But we do want to help them view the worldly situation *theologically.* Of course, what goes on in a classroom is really out of our hands. There may be all kinds of heresy spouted in our classrooms, along with smugness and self-righteousness. But we believe that in the Christian faith there is a 'given.' Somehow we must help our folks to face the world, but to face it as the people of God."

If courses in ethics would accomplish this goal, the mission of the church in the world would soon be achieved. Forcefully written, attractively illustrated, theologically sound paperbacks, dealing with poverty, parenthood, race, and vocation, were being published and discussed in almost every denomination. The Uniform Lessons were designed to begin with scripture, and it was easy for a group to bog down in the eighth century B.C. and never get to "applying the lesson to life." Elective courses gave the class the option of not choosing to look at controversial issues. But the new curricula, if bought as a package, did virtually force the Protestant Sunday school class to a theological consideration of ethical issues in the contemporary world. Only the more left-wing theologians were likely to charge the curriculum planners with lack of ethical concern. It was not equally clear that the classroom discussions would prove completely effective.

Modern Methods

In the Johnsonian "era of consensus" in which most of the curricula were produced the Protestant bureaucrats appeared to have achieved also a large measure of agreement about methods.

1. The most obvious commitment was to the study-discussion method. Research is still somewhat ambiguous as to the relative merits of lecture *vs.* discussion, though it must be agreed that most adult educators do prefer discussion for attitudinal change.[9] I personally, at least, have never seen in a denominational manual any reference to the research projects which reported no significant difference between the two approaches. Rather, there seemed to be unanimous agreement that discussion is to be preferred. Here is one example from a guide for teachers in the Lutheran Church in America:

Each chapter ends with a question or a series of questions, not with a summary or a set of instructions on how to act. This has an important bearing on the way you conduct discussions. It means that the teacher *should not summarize,* should not hand out a set of conclusions at the end of his teaching period. You must not concern yourself primarily with giving answers: your chief role will be to ask questions.[10]

Though it carefully warned against continuing to follow this time schedule inflexibility, a United Church of Christ manual outlined a step-by-step Bible study pattern which was typical of those being advocated in many denominations, sometimes with the title "Depth Bible Study":

     5 minutes: Opening prayer or hymn
     5 minutes: Getting into focus, introduction
   15 minutes: Discussion. What did this passage

say to its day? (This includes the reading of the passage and the commentary in the lesson material and discussion of questions about its original meaning.)

10 minutes: Discussion. What does it say to us today?

10 minutes: Discussion. What new light has come to us from our study?

10 minutes: Discussion. What are we to do about it?

Dr. C. Ellis Nelson warned that such study could become a "simplified neo-pietist hermeneutic." "It tends to bypass such questions as the literary form of a passage, its historical setting, and the insights of centuries of intervening history. And it tries to cover too much in a limited time schedule."

"We feel that meaty resources commonly experienced are the key to worthwhile discussion," Prof. Richard T. Murray, of Perkins School of Theology, told me about the Methodist curriculum for adults being introduced in 1967. "Our trouble in the past has been that too often we have talked about what we've thought but not about other people's ideas. To help the discussion really get somewhere we're proposing to give every class member not only the book of readings but the study guide. This means that there is no separate book for the teachers. This may seem threatening to some leaders, and we may even lose some. But we really are serious about this business of shared participation."

Obviously, such concentration on participation by the group members has necessitated new leadership training programs. "We think of printed materials as only one fourth of our new curriculum plans," the Rev. Edward Power of the United Church of Christ staff stated. "Another fourth is the new media. And half is leadership training." By the mid-1960's the Lutheran Church in America was experimenting with various types of laboratory schools for teachers of adults. Other groups were seeking in various ways to involve class members themselves through such programs as the Indiana Plan, the Parish Life Conferences of the Episcopal Church, the 12-Hour Adult Workshops of the Presbyterian Church, U. S., or the Mission 12 Groups of the Church of the Brethren. Their theory was, in part, that good discussion requires skill not only of the leader but of the participants themselves.

2. A remarkable variety of audio-visuals was an important part of the new study resources. Recorded plays of six minutes each could now be pressed, one on each side of a seven-inch disk, and marketed for a quarter. Thus a Covenant Life Curriculum class studying church history might actually "tune in" on an imaginary you-are-there broadcast of the Council of Nicaea. *Patterns of the Mind,* a movie used to help introduce the new curriculum of the Lutheran Church in America, brought filmed interviews with leading scientists into the classrooms of many denominations. It was but one of hundreds of new motion pictures. The Episcopalians pioneered in the production of poster series for classroom use. The Covenant Life Curriculum reproduced great paintings for one church history course. The new Method-

ist curriculum included poster-sized comic cartoons. Though no denominational publisher had done so yet, an independent house who produced a rather conservative curriculum especially popular among Lutherans in the Midwest, had actually developed a series of lesson pictures for adults comparable to those used for many years with children. Filmstrips, however, were supplemented with nine- or ten-frame film clips for quick visualization of something being studied. And new forms of equipment, designed for use with small study groups, were manufactured by various producers. A Methodist editor reported that a Florida minister was lecturing to the classes in his church each Sunday over closed-circuit television. The lectures were then followed by small group discussions.

3. The American Lutherans pioneered in taking seriously the notion of discipline in a denominationally promoted program of study. As one part of their PACE program each church was asked to encourage the formation of "encounter groups," to be restricted to four couples each, whose members would covenant:

> to meet together once a month for a determined number of months;
>
> to study faithfully;
>
> to cooperate in group process;
>
> to attend church services regularly;
>
> to have daily private or family devotions;
>
> to pray daily for the congregation, the pastor, and each other;
>
> to help uphold one another in the Spirit of Christ;

> to dissolve the group following a predetermined number of meetings;
>
> to assist in the forming of new groups.

At the time of this writing it was not yet apparent how many would accept this kind of challenge or how widely the American Lutheran's experiment would be imitated. It seemed eminently worth exploring.

Some Problems and Possibilities

Certainly the effort at renewal through adult education deserved to be recorded as one of the most massive programs in the history of American Protestantism. In terms of money spent, prayers prayed, care in planning, and the number of people involved, perhaps nothing before had ever been comparable for the training of the laity. How effective an instrument of the Holy Spirit the Protestant curricula of the 60's would prove to be, perhaps only their consequences in the 70's would indicate. Perhaps no one but God would ever know.

Certain limitations of the curricula were apparent from the beginning.

"Look," said one minister in a metropolitan church when I inquired why he did not use his denominational curriculum, "how far ahead do you have to plan that stuff? Two years? Three years?"

I confessed the whole process took more like seven.

"Man," he replied, "we can't plan more than six months in advance. If we did, we'd be dead. Last year civil rights was the thing. We could get two hundred people out on a Sunday for a good program on civil rights. This year I'll bet we couldn't get fifty." (This was in 1966.) "This year 'God-is-dead' is the thing. We try to study the newspapers and the magazines to find out what these people are reading in the religion section of *Time* or any section of the newspapers. We couldn't possibly use things dealing with the questions people were asking five years ago."

I mumbled some reply about the dangers in letting the editors of *Time* and *Life* control the church's teaching ministry, but I knew he had a point. Indeed, the incident about the three *Mighty Acts of God* illustrated it even in the relatively stable concern of Bible study. By 1964, when these volumes were being studied, the emphasis in biblical theology was so changed that, had they been written a year or two later, it is possible that none would have been given exactly that title.

The curriculum planners, of course, are not unaware of the problem. "The deadline on *Trends* [a magazine published ten times a year for Presbyterians, Episcopalians, and the United Church of Christ] is three months in advance," says Jack Worthington of the United Presbyterians, "but we can get something in on shorter notice if we have to." The American Lutherans were able to publish guides for theological analysis of films which could be used while the movies were still in the neighborhood theaters. Good writers of curriculum books were as capable of producing literature of contemporary relevance as were those who wrote for other publishers. Few in the United Church of Christ or in other denominations studying in 1966 Byron L. Johnson's *Need Is Our*

Neighbor [11] felt it was out of date in the midst of the then newly proclaimed national "war on poverty." Yet the inevitable time lag did form one reason for the need for creativity at the local level.

Perhaps a more serious problem was that the curricula were of necessity published to sell in a mass market. This meant that they had to be beamed toward the average church member. But a curriculum that is effective for the white middle-class suburban striver may miss completely the slum-dweller or the coal miner.

Again the curriculum planners are more familiar with the problem than confident of solution. Representatives from five major denominations met in Atlantic City in the fall of 1965 to hear Jack E. Weller, author of *Yesterday's People*,[12] and Charles S. Sydnor, outstanding mission worker in the Appalachian region, explain why their denominational curricula were virtually useless in their mining camp churches. With the time lag it will be well into the 1970's before the curriculum planners provide the resources likely to be developed as the result of the survey of the Appalachian religious education problems begun in 1967. Special curricula for the inner city were being produced by independent or local interdenominational groups, but the denominations generally had not in the 60's devised materials fully meeting the needs of slum-dwelling adults.

A third problem has already been alluded to. Some would charge that the denominational curricula are too much the product of the ecclesiastical establishment and too much designed to appeal to the mass consensus ever to lead prophetically to a renewal of the church. A curriculum plan such as the Cooperative Curriculum Project based on a theory of the development of self was certain to sound too individualistic and self-centered to those who would emphasize "education for mission in the world."

Fourth, many would charge that the very structure and methodology of the whole Protestant adult education enterprise prevented any real encounter with the world. In 1964 Marshall McLuhan had taught all who were interested in communication his famous axiom, "The medium is the message." [13] The medium of the older approach to adult education was to get a group of people together and have them listen to a lecture. The newer approach was an improvement—to get a group of people together and have them discuss. But inevitably the discussion group might tend to suggest that the goal of Christian education is words, not deeds.

Finally, the curricula of the 60's, complete, balanced, and slickly packaged and marketed, ran the risk of being so thoroughgoing and attractive that they would stifle creativity at the local level where creativity was equally important.

Again curriculum planners were painfully aware of the danger. Indeed, they were eager to encourage congregations to plan for themselves. "When churches ask us the ideal, we come back with 'Study your adults,'" protests Gideon Wick of the Lutheran Church in America. "We ask them to find out what their members need and when they are available for study, and then to pick studies appropriate to their own situation." "Our whole approach used to be to get everybody in one program," Fred Schenk, west coast American Lutheran educator, put it. "That didn't work. Now we are recognizing that people are different. That's why PACE offers four options." "We're not saying this is *it,*" agrees the United Presbyterians' Ed Trefz. "Curriculum must be created locally." Indeed, one curriculum writer paused from his labors long enough to propose to me privately that "it's a crime to keep grinding out more study books. There are enough good ones in print already. The need is to help churches use what's already available."

The Protestant Episcopal Church produced in 1967 a volume entitled *A Book, a Group, and You,* designed to help teachers use for group study any of the books already at hand. Every introductory program —perhaps especially the Methodist materials looking toward "a new day"—contained detailed suggestions for surveying the local congregation and planning specifically in the light of its needs. Yet it could not be denied that the new curricula provided a crutch for those who simply wanted something to lean on.

Fully aware of these difficulties, few curriculum planners had illusions about the winning of the world —or even the church—for Christ in their generation through their own efforts. A standard joke around one bureaucracy was to schedule out the coming events: leadership training, preparation of the church, introductory year, first cycle, and then—the *parousia,* the *millennium,* and the *eschaton.* The text most often quoted was not an eschatological passage but the proverb "Of making many books there is no end, and much study is a weariness of the flesh." Only the advertising brochures were likely to imply that a new curriculum would bring in the kingdom.

And yet, most curriculum planners I have met have seemed to approach their work not only with obvious dedication but with a real sense of expectancy and excitement. Let it be granted that study alone was not all that the church needed. Still it was one significant place to begin. Let it be granted again that some of the materials were excellent, and some were duds. By and large, the books were gospel centered, attractive, and balanced. "If we never put out any books at all, it would be worth the effort," one planner commented in the midst of production. "The discussion of the new curriculum has caused so many churches to restudy their whole programs." The massive leadership training programs brought new depth of study in many places. And the prospect of some millions of Protestants taking a fresh look in new ways at God's Word and viewing God's world in the light of that Word in ways never attempted before made the enterprise seem one to which many could willingly devote their lives.

4

CREATIVITY
IN THE
CONGREGATION

"Let us go forth . . . outside the camp."

Back in the 40's Ethel Merman had taught the world to respond to a challenge by singing, "Anything you can do, I can do better!" Though all too few in number, there were here and there throughout the nation congregations which had adopted a similar attitude toward the more radical renewal projects of the 60's. The Church of the Saviour had pioneered in establishing a novel form of Christian witness, a coffee house. By 1965 there were one thousand church-sponsored coffee houses around the country. Judson Memorial had explored the relationship of Christianity and the arts. One could soon find church drama groups in Atlanta and church-sponsored art festivals in Oklahoma. At the Ecumenical Institute in Chicago "vanward students" studied Paul Tillich and Dietrich Bonhoeffer. So did Methodists in Greensboro, North Carolina, and Episcopalians in Baltimore.

Indeed, not all the encounter with the world which was taking place in established churches was in imitation of the renewal centers. Several suburban congregations had come up with fresh ideas of their own. Some were not very successful. Some, it was charged, were negated by the very fact of their context in suburbia. But they were a factor to be reckoned with by those who were ready to predict, sometimes with apparent hope, that the established church was dying.

The greatest challenge which the prophets of renewal had proposed was that the churches needed to take seriously the world in which they were called to minister. This chapter will describe some ways in which the adult education programs of many churches were trying to deal responsibly with the twentieth century.

Serious Study of Ethical Issues

The most common way in which churches tried to face the contemporary world was the most nearly traditional: group study of Christian ethics.

We have already noted how hundreds of congregations had wrestled with the biting attacks on suburbia found in such curriculum texts as Waldo Beach's *The Christian Life* or had tried to face the implications of the statistics on poverty in mission study books such as Byron L. Johnson's *Need Is Our Neighbor.* "The denominational curriculum—that pious pap?" a progressive-minded minister once exclaimed when I asked him if he had found the new texts useful. I was not surprised, however, to find that he simply had not seen the kind of books his church was producing lately. The new texts did not, of course, make retreat into the "good old days" impossible for the average Sunday school class. They did make possible a potent option.

Many churches, however, did not confine their choices to texts mass produced by the denominations. The adults of the Barrington, Vermont, Congregational Church tackled John Bennett's controversial *Foreign Policy in Perspective.* At a time when it was still regarded, in some circles at least, as unpatriotic to question the country's militant stand in Vietnam, the Methodists in Mamaroneck, New York, were spending Sunday evenings studying the problem. Though civil disobedience may have been accepted as a respected form of protest in many parts of the country, it took some courage for Centenary Methodist Church to advertise a forum on the subject in the mid-60's in Winston-Salem, North Carolina. In 1965 an audience which was 99 percent white followed an address by the late Martin Luther King with a standing ovation at the Southern Presbyterian conference grounds at Montreat, North Carolina. Armed police stood guard outside the meeting in view of the racial tensions then still likely to bring violence in the South. In days to come the newsletters of a thousand congregations would document perhaps less dramatic but sincere efforts to view contemporary history from a theological perspective.

Attacking Community Problems

Studies of particular communities suggested more immediate responsibilities of a highly controversial nature. Examples of church groups taking a hard look at their hometowns were not common. But such study did go on.

Bartenders in Louisville were no doubt startled one February afternoon in 1965 by little groups of adult Christian educators asking them questions about their work. Simultaneously, similar interviews were being held in factories and real estate agencies. The adult section of the annual Christian Education Conference of the National Council of Churches had had its quota of lectures about what "the world" thinks of the church. One afternoon they divided into little groups and went out to find out for themselves. Some descended on department stores. Some talked with politicians. Reports next day indicated reactions of amazement even in places where arrangements for their visits had been carefully made in advance. "They feel that the church doesn't understand what they are up against," one visitor reported, "and they were surprised that we even wanted to understand." By 1967 groups at a similar convention were even visiting a Dallas, Texas, bar which was popular with homosexuals. Inevitably, the National Council experiments were to lead to similar smaller projects.

Storm Lake, Iowa, for example, is a county seat. A Presbyterian synod leadership training program departed from the lecture-discussion formula and sent its participants to interview the chief of police, the editor of the town paper, a sanitation official, businessmen, and the president of the Chamber of Commerce. "I don't know whether we could have done this had we not been from out of town," admits United Presbyterian executive Ed Trefz. "Some of the questions were pretty loaded." But the activity symbolized a new direction in leadership training.

Some churches, however, have taken a hard look at their own hometowns. First Presbyterian Church, Cedar Falls, Iowa, had the candidates for mayor, a county welfare representative, and young people from a Negro housing area to address their adult study group. Often community impact has necessitated the cooperation of a number of churches. "My congregation in the suburbs can't really alter the life of our city," a South Carolina pastor told me. "To do that we've got to work with others."

A notable effort was that of the Wilton (Connecticut) Ecumenical Center. Here Congregationalists, Episcopalians, Methodists, Presbyterians, and Friends shared in forums which involved such touchy issues as a referendum on the parochial school bus issue (in which Roman Catholic representatives participated). The Wilton Ecumenical Center advertised itself as part of the renewal movement, seeking to relate that challenge to the life of a suburban community. With headquarters in the village shopping-center area the program has produced for the local paper a weekly column, sometimes controversial, and has attempted such specific service projects as a summer job registry for youth. Discussions have included dialogue with Roman Catholics and Jews, analysis of the new Connecticut Constitution, and consideration of regional planning in the area. In 1966 the Center helped begin a regional ecumenical project to coordinate "the public ministries" of eight similiar towns in the area.

The Fairchester Project in the same area has made use of denominational structures by involving seven suburban Presbyterian churches. Project studies have focused on church-related problems characteristic of suburbia—the way the success drive enslaves businessmen, for example. There is a course taught by a mobile teaching team beamed at the problem of transient church membership in mobile America. More closely related, perhaps, to "worldly" concerns, the project was digging into the question of fair housing in the area and considering possible racial and economic discrimination. The session of one of the participating churches, First Presbyterian of Stamford, officially went on record in the fall of 1966 as endorsing the principle of scattering low-cost housing throughout its community. Again, one suspects that there may have been some accompanying controversy where residents may have perceived such discussions as a threat to their property values.

The Twin Cities Area Town Meeting of November, 1966, attempted to educate for civic responsibility the citizens of a quite different metropolis, Minneapolis and St. Paul, Minnesota. Relying heavily on television and other mass media, this huge effort involved thirty identical briefing sessions in schools, shopping centers, and churches, use of the distinguished TV series "Metropolis—Creator or Destroyer?" films, and numerous small discussion groups led by moderators especially trained at the University of Minnesota. The Higher Education Act of 1965 provided a grant which defrayed some of the expenses of this massive civic and religious enterprise. Subjects for which discussion manuals were provided included "Government," "Designing a Human City," "Ghettos in the City: Aged, Racial, Economic," "Youth and the Future of the City," etc.

First Community Church, Columbus, Ohio, was sufficiently involved as a congregation in activities related to its city that it employed a "minister to the public sector."

An Accent on the Arts

The 50's rediscovered the word *kergyma*. The 60's preferred to talk about "dialogue." The church's task, we were assured, was not simply to proclaim but also to listen. It was a well-nigh creedal dogma of the renewal prophets that "the world must write the agenda." It was natural, therefore, that congregations would begin to take seriously what was being said by those who most eloquently expressed the world's values—the artists.

If one elbowed his way through the bearded or mini-skirted teen-agers of the Greenwich Village art colony on a Saturday night to Judson Memorial Church, he would likely find a play in progress. He could also find this in the fashionable suburban Trinity Presbyterian Church in Atlanta. I watched near-professional performances in the cathedral-like Riverside Church in New York. "The Bishop's Company" toured the nation, performing secular plays in sacred surroundings. "We are expecting to offer the services of our drama group to neighboring congregations," the Rev. Ray Brown of Lexington, Kentucky, told me. "But on one condition: they must use them at eleven o'clock on Sunday morning. We don't want our drama to be just a sideshow."

Listening to the world was not confined to do-it-yourself thespians and their audiences. Hollywood films were being seen in a new light. At the end of 1966 Protestants and Catholics joined to present their own version of the "Oscar" to movies of special merit —the Protestants carefully selecting *Who's Afraid of Virginia Woolf,* a film whose language in an earlier era would have produced calls for censorship in such pious circles. And from Carolina to California congregations were converting sanctuaries into cinemas and then discussing Hollywood features from the standpoint of theological analysis. At St. Clement's Episcopal Church, New York, a playbill might be injected into the prayer book at the Sunday worship. The recently formed St. Clement's Film Society listed old Hollywood movies which were useful for churches around the country; it also produced discussion guides. "Mass Media Ministries" published biweekly a review of available films and upcoming TV programs of special interest to churches around the nation. The aim was by no means simply entertainment but serious analysis of the ethical and even theological issues raised by such movies.

For example, in one fall season members of the West Market Street Methodist Church of Greensboro, North Carolina, on successive Sunday evenings watched Gregory Peck in *To Kill a Mockingbird*, Van Heflin in *Patterns*, Keir Dullea in *David and Lisa*, and Marlon Brando in *On the Waterfront*. The series concluded with Anthony Quinn in *Zorba the Greek*. In each case the film showing was followed by discussion which sought to relate the slice of world the film had pictured to the faith the church proclaimed.

Some critics lamented that Protestantism over the years had seemed to lose contact with all the arts except architecture. There were churches, however, where groups were sincerely seeking to involve themselves in dialogue with the arts. An outstanding example was the First Presbyterian Church of Tulsa, Oklahoma. They began in 1961 an annual "Christ in the Arts" festival series which included special musical activities, drama study and presentations, and a religious art display. Works of artists from various parts of the country and from their own congregation and community have been used, with paintings, wood, metal, and earthen sculpture, and what minister of music James S. Boles calls "a multitude of various art media." "Our purpose in these shows," Mr. Boles wrote me, "has not been to award prizes, not to offer judgment, but to encourage professional and amateur artists to express themselves in matters relating to their faith . . . and to share this expression with members of our own congregation and community." The National Gallery of Art, Washington, D. C., prepared a special display for one showing, to which were added paintings loaned by the Christian Art Company of California.

My brother, Prof. Charles M. Ramsay, took a group of students to see a contrasting kind of art at Dallas' Satori House, where a Methodist pastor with Presbyterian support ministered to young adults, including hippies. The program began with "a light show, a very weird performance, featuring a dazzling display of lights with guitar music and some contortionist dancers, after which there was a rather long theological discussion in just about the most unusual surroundings I have ever seen for the Christian gospel," he reported.

Sometimes the church's efforts at educational dialogue with the arts seemed inartistic, but there was certainly a new and hopeful effort.

Task and Mission Groups

Such renewal churches as the Church of the Saviour in Washington and Christ Church, Presbyterian, in Burlington, Vermont, had raised the question as to whether or not education programs have not reversed the proper order. We have discussed and studied, hoping this would lead to action. Their approach has been to act and to find that this leads to discussion.

The new Presbyterian Church of the Apostles, Burnsville, Minnesota, adopted the same approach.

Every new group of candidates for church membership was expected to become an "apostles group." These groups were involved weekly or bimonthly in regular work at the county mental health clinic or the state children's hospital, in gathering clothes for the Delta Ministry, or in some similar activity. Regular study was a part of the program of each apostles group, too, but it was clearly understood that each group existed for ministry, with the study simply a means of equipment for their work.

The Village Presbyterian Church in a suburb of Kansas City had attempted to adapt this pattern to the life of an older congregation. A call was issued for members who were willing to participate in disciplined "parish in the world" teams. Some one hundred agreed to share in these groups for a period of a year. Prepared with several introductory sessions and a weekend retreat for all, training group members now agreed to spend one evening a week, or its equivalent, in yearlong mission projects. These included work with youth in the inner city, the "12 + 1" coffee house, work with older adults, and a vocational study group. Books by Dietrich Bonhoeffer and C. S. Lewis were texts. Though he was cautious at first, minister of education Donald M. Parkinson, after more than a year of experiment, wrote me about the parish in the world approach: "We feel we are far enough along to recommend its use to others."

It must be said, however, that this kind of task grouping—working first and studying second—was still a rarity in the Protestantism of the 1960's.

96

Vocational Groups

"Church Seeks Wall St. 'Dialogue,'" said the headlines of an article in the *New York Times* of February 6, 1967:

What are the most serious pressures placed upon a securities salesman? What values do bankers employ in their decision-making? What are the meanings and long-range goals of business life?

Men and women of all faiths in the Wall Street area will soon be encouraged to discuss such questions, geared to actual problems. The impetus will come from the Wall Street Ministry, a new group formed to bring "the churches and the financial community into dialogue." ...

"Small group discussion will be our stock in trade," explained the Reverend Francis C. Huntington. . . . The "dialogue" will take place in company rooms and in the small headquarters office of the ministry at 55 Liberty Street, a short walk from the New York Stock Exchange.

Obviously, American churches were beginning to get something of the message of the lay academies of Europe. The Wall Street Ministry, sponsored primarily by the Episcopalians and the United Church of Christ, was only one among several vocationally oriented efforts. Their theory was that the church did not need to set up special opportunities for ministry in the world. Most lay people are already in the world. The task is to help them relate their faith directly to the work in which they are already involved.

Scientists and Engineers for Social Action (SESA) was formed in San Francisco, bringing together a group of west coast scientists to study and act on problems related to the technological revolution. Highland Park Methodist Church, Dallas, Texas, had regular meetings of its physicians in which they discussed such questions as the counseling of unmarried girls who are pregnant. The Presbyterian Church, U. S., Men of the Church and Women of the Church joined forces to sponsor an experimental "lay school" for barbers and beauticians. "We didn't know the church was that interested in *us!*" one participant exclaimed.

The Project in Vocation in Little Rock, Arkansas, brought together such groups as dentists, letter carriers, and teachers. "Our dentists were ready to talk about individual problems," reports director William Holshouser, "but they tended to pull back from discussing collective issues involving laws or the dental association."

One of the most remarkable vocational projects was the Experimental Study of Religion and Society, led by Dr. Donald W. Shriver, Jr., of the Presbyterian Church, U. S. Using the unusual academic resources of Raleigh, Durham, and Chapel Hill, North Carolina (North Carolina State, Duke University, and the University of North Carolina) , and supported in part by a grant from a foundation, the program has drawn together professors, businessmen, and statesmen for high-level discussions concerning the life of the state. Twelve physical and biological scientists, four theologians, one professor of history, and one philosopher focused monthly on intellectual and moral issues faced by the scientist in his vocation. Ten presidents, or managers of major industrial enterprises, two economists, and three theologians engaged in extended discussions of executive decision-making. Eight politicians and administrative officers, an editor, three theologians, and four other politically active persons formed another of Shriver's groups.

While other examples could be named, it should be admitted frankly that Christian educators of the 60's still found vocational groups hard to establish. One could document cases where projects failed for lack of participants. I myself have seen near terror in a business executive's eyes and heard the defensiveness in his voice as the possibility of a retreat for high-level business leaders was proposed to him. Most of the examples already mentioned, though all are from church-sponsored projects, are not from single congregations acting alone. Vocational groupings were still an exception in adult education in the 1960's.

Partnership Projects

Sociologically oriented Gibson Winter put his finger on a basic problem, *The Suburban Captivity of the Churches*. The typical Protestant church member, living and worshiping in a relatively affluent suburb, was sheltered from the real world of poverty by the very structure which tried to teach him concern for the poor. One of Winter's proposals was a "sector plan" which would bring together church members across racial and class lines. Something akin to this was being tried in a number of places, as more affluent congregations strengthened the ties which bound them to brothers in the inner city.

Inner-city missions, some inspired by the East Harlem Parish and similar projects, were springing up all over the country. The women who left Shades Valley Church on the edge of Birmingham to help with a summer remedial school in less fortunate Handley Memorial Church were genuinely helping others. Incidentally, they were also receiving an adult education.

"The first thing we had to do was to admit we hated each other," Dr. Carlyle Marney once remarked as he described a meeting of representatives of Myers Park Baptist Church in Charlotte, North Carolina, and a Negro Baptist church in the same city. "But we had a lot to learn from each other, too."

In such encounters, of course, there is always need to guard against the danger of paternalism. That is why the congregations of one suburban church and the Sea and Land Methodist-Presbyterian Church in a less affluent New York area worked on the suburban church's lawn together. "It may seem silly," commented student minister Hugh McMillan of Sea and Land, "but the fact that we were all mowing their grass together kept it from being just a matter of their doing something for us. It really meant a lot to our congregation to feel instead that we were helping them." Perhaps the church has a unique opportunity to achieve such direct contact between the inner city and the suburb.

Families

There were three areas of traditional concern for adult education which were not generally high on the agenda of the renewal projects. Yet each did have special problems related to life in the twentieth century, and churches were undertaking new forms of ministry to these segments of society. The three were families, older adults, and younger adults.

It is true that some questioned whether a ministry focused on families still had relevance for the modern world. Letty Russell, for example, found that in Harlem the function of the Church of the Ascension was, in part, to serve as a kind of substitute for the family. The traditional household, including a loving father for every child, simply did not exist. The United Presbyterians finally abandoned the approach to the home through numerous magazines for parents, one of the outstanding features of their original Christian Faith and Life Curriculum. Nevertheless, most children still were born into families in the 1960's. At one time or another in their lives most women regarded motherhood as their chief concern. And there were still millions of Christian men having some concern for and seeking help with their responsibilities as husbands and parents.

Continued efforts to help adults in the area of family living did not mean that churches were entirely unaware of the contrast between the modern home and that of Grandmother's day. A poster for use with a Covenant Life Curriculum study was in the form of an old-fashioned cross-stitched sampler, but its satirical motto read "God bless our cafeteria and dormitory!" One leaflet indicated the state of family life in the 60's with such figures as these:

33% of the labor force are women, 78% of whom are mothers;

5.8 million children live with only one parent;

30% of teen-aged brides are pregnant;

Venereal disease is contacted by 250,000 teen-agers annually.

Ministry to families, which of course included ministry to children and youth as well as adults, lies beyond the narrow scope of this book, meriting a volume of its own. It should be noted, however, that every curriculum, including the new one of the United Presbyterians, tried in one way or another to assist adults in their family responsibilities. And beyond these curricula one could find hundreds of churches attempting in various fashions to train their laity for this ministry.

Here are a few examples of projects from among the many available: The Open School, drawing students from many churches but sponsored by the Church of the Redeemer and St. Matthew's Episcopal Church in Baltimore, offered in one winter such courses as "Our Young Americans" for parents of teen-agers, "To Know and Believe," for parents of younger children, and "The Modern Family" and "The Christian and the Crisis of Sex" for couples.

Second Presbyterian Church, Knoxville, Tennessee, had earlier set up a lay counseling program, training selected lay members to visit and counsel families in the congregation assigned to the care of each.

West Market Street Methodist, Greensboro, North Carolina, making an ally of commercial television, centered one discussion around a documentary on ABC entitled "Sex in the Sixties."

Older Adults

By 1966 there were 18.5 million Americans over the age of sixty-five. The number will probably reach 24.5 million by the end of the 70's. A high percentage of these were poor. Though not always highlighted in the renewal literature, they constituted a group with whom the churches had opportunity. Many congregations had devised new ways of meeting the growing challenge.

St. Luke's Methodist Church in Oklahoma City packed old people into six or eight simultaneous weekday classes, operating from nine to twelve and from two to four, with a 75-cent lunch served in between. Four fifths of the students and three fourths of the teachers came from outside the church congregation. The four most popular courses centered on Bible, investments, travel, and world problems, but piano, crafts, archaeology, and languages were included. The report told of one student who had lost interest in a prepaid funeral policy as he became involved in the program!

The First Baptist Church of Los Angeles offered monthly trips, usually at a cost of less than five dollars, courses in the arts and in lipreading. The church has worked in cooperation with the Cambria Adult School of the Los Angeles public school system, with instructors from the city school system coming to the church to teach courses in international affairs, American problems, or music.

"We have around 3,500 members at Riverside," says the Rev. James Farmer, "but we figure we minister to some 15,000 people." One reason this New York church has reached so many is because of its three-pronged program aimed at older people who are still relatively independent, at those who can manage with a minimum of assistance, and at those who need a great amount of professional help. One 1965 series of studies, which drew national attention and an editorial in the *New York Times,* focused directly on the subject of death and the problems related to it.

The First Methodist Church of Baton Rouge, Louisiana, has built a new adult center with a capacity of seven hundred to house its five-day weekly program for senior citizens.

The activities of these four congregations seemed significant enough that the United States Department of Health, Education, and Welfare in 1965 published *Brighter Vistas,* a booklet describing them.

Younger Adults

Perhaps the denominationally sponsored program which most squarely faced the world of today was, significantly, the one which broke most completely out of the old settings. For adult education at its most modern, one could find no more revolutionary example with which to close this chapter than the Methodist-related Young Adult Project. With a ministry ranging from high-rise apartments to homosexual bars, the project seemed, to some at least, the prototype in the 60's of what the church must become in the 1970's.

The young adult classes, whose enrollment had mushroomed after World War II, were steadily dwindling by the time of the Vietnam conflict. Though thousands of churches still had young adult fellowships patterned after the traditional youth fellowship model, this movement, too, was no longer booming. Yet the number of Americans between the ages of eighteen and twenty-four rose 64 percent in the decade of the 60's. Flocking to the cities, these youth made up as much as one third of several census tracts in such rapidly spreading metropolises as Dallas.

In San Francisco it was estimated that less than 5 percent of the younger adults were related to any church in any way.

Let us be clear (wrote the directors of the project, Charles E. Mowry and Earl R. Williford): We contend there is in America today a distinct and, in many ways self-contained young adult culture. This new culture will not pass away. Nor will the persons in it gradually become like us as they grow older. They are a new kind of person who lives in a new age and generally judges our age—its ways, its piety, and its institutions—as either inadequate or irrelevant.[1]

Ministry to that culture in such a city as San Francisco has necessitated breaking out of the "Pairs and Spares Club" mold. Since these youth do not go to church, the church has sought to go to them, expressing its concern in ways they can understand.

In San Francisco, for example, it was found that

young adults seek counsel not so much from priests and ministers as from their apartment house managers. Those participating in the project helped sponsor a course in counseling for apartment managers, getting help from social agencies and psychologists. Recognizing how many young newcomers to the city did not know where to turn for help of various kinds, they published a "Directory of Community Resources for Young Adults" and placed it for distribution in hotels, restaurants, and coffee houses. They provided one special housing facility for thirty young men and women to help them in their first adjustment to the city. With the United Presbyterians and the United Church of Christ the Methodists worked through Precarious Vision, a coffee house, using it as a forum for examining problems of contemporary life and for studying the relationship of religion and the fine arts. And they have even dared in compassion to seek out homosexuals, helping to establish the Council on Religion and Homosexuality in San Francisco.

Begun by the Methodists, the project in the second half of the decade began attracting the support of other denominations. Interdenominationally sponsored conferences of church and community leaders were projected for many cities in the nation in 1967 and the years following, with the stated goal "to put the young adult on the agenda of the cities of America." Presumably, projects comparable to that of San Francisco might become common in the 70's.

Bureaucrat that he was, Charles E. Mowry, then chairman of the National Council's Committee on

Young Adult Work, wrote of the committee project in terms that showed a real unity with "the renewal movement":

The present generation of young adults are getting most of their communications from the church through *what we do or fail to do that affects their lives directly.* This plan is designed to respond faithfully to the historic task of Christians, namely to show love and concern for the state and experience of our neighbor. . . . The method of ministry of the church has always been to go where men are. This is the root of the incarnation event—God acting in the midst of men. This plan calls for the church to act, in the name of God, in the midst of a generation of men and women.[2]

5

SOME
PREDICTIONS
AND PROPOSALS

"It does not yet appear what we shall be."

As we lunched in the cafeteria of the Inter-Church Center in New York, I asked Carl Williams, now a professor but at that time the staff member of the National Council of Churches most closely associated with adult education, to summarize the current trends as an administrator sees them.

"I see four," he suggested. "First, adults today are doing more serious study. The new curricula are not pablum. Churches are involving their adults in the study of some of the most serious books written in this century. I don't mean that the study now going on is all we could hope for. But there is some real study." (Chapter III documented this thesis.)

"Second," he continued, "there is still a strong trend toward informal study in small discussion groups." (Chapter II noted some origins of this trend.)

"Third, there is a greater concern about participation in community structures by adult Christians. There are signs that adults are taking seriously their mission in the world." (Chapters I and IV noted at least a few places where this is clearly true.)

"Finally," said Mr. Williams, "I have been interested to note the rise of adult Christian education as a subject of graduate study. For example, there is the notable program at the University of Indiana." (One listing of the courses given in thirty schools offering degrees or majors in Christian education indicated that twenty-five had courses with the word "adult" in the title.)

I went to the office of Dean Kendig Brubaker Cully of New York Theological Seminary for a professor's slant. "I would hesitate to predict the future," Dr. Cully demurred. "But certainly there is currently a strong emphasis on the behavioral sciences, especially sociology." (Chapter I noted the influence of sociologists on the renewal movement.)

Over coffee I asked Dr. Pieter de Jong, professor of systematic theology at the same seminary, what would be studied in curricula ten years from now. "Are you sure there are going to be any more new curricula?" he said. "My understanding has been that the emphasis on new materials has proved a bit disappointing. Aren't most churches putting the stress now on leadership training?" (I remembered that Edward Power had said that the Board of the United Church of Christ thinks of leadership training as half the job.)

In one sense it would seem that accurate predictions regarding the future of Christian adult education ought to be easily made. Hindsight indicates that someone familiar with the writings of Gerhard von Rad, G. Ernest Wright, and Bernhard W. Anderson might have predicted the trinity of *Mighty Acts* ten years before they appeared. Indeed, according to one secular educator, there is typically a thirty-five-to-fifty-year gap between the time an idea is first conceived and the time it is fully spread throughout the public schools.[1] Religious education is no further behind than that, but there is enough of a lag that it might seem that prophecies could be accurate. "The trouble is," says C. Ellis Nelson, "that there are too many things going on. You can never be sure which idea is going to come out as the dominant one."

Nevertheless, one prediction seems safe: certain of the conflicts which we have noted throughout the history of Christian education are likely to continue. Indeed, as one reads the works of the secular prophets who protest the failures of the public schools—Paul Goodman, for example—one senses that these conflicts are not confined to religious education.

We have noted such repeated themes as the following: the conflict of a free lay movement with institutionalism; the conflict of progress with tradition; the strong thrust of the Spirit in the direction of the perceived need of the moment *vs.* the desire for balance and order; activism *vs.* intellectualism; concern with the society *vs.* concern with the individual; and liberal concern for doctrinal relevance *vs.* conservative emphasis on doctrinal purity. Each of these has appeared in different forms at different times. It is, perhaps, the surest prediction one can make concerning the future of Protestant adult education that these tensions are likely to appear again, as cycles repeat themselves.

Rushing in where any professor fears to tread, I would add the following predictions.

The Trend Toward Flexibility

Even before the last of the new curricula appeared, there was a discernible trend away from structured curricula for adults. To this observer it seems unlikely that the 1970's will see the production of many more huge programs, carefully planned and packaged at the national level for mass consumption at the grass roots. The new curricula have served a worthy purpose. But they themselves had sought in various ways to develop greater creativity at the local level. In the cycle of history the elective idea seems likely to come to new life again in the decade ahead, aided by new resources and greater help in planning.

The 1968 report of the Policy and Procedures Committee of the Department of Education for Mission of the National Council of Churches announced plans for gradual abandonment of the annual mission study theme. The statement summarized the trend and the reasons for it in part in these words:

We are now in a creative and changing period in the life of the church. The church engaged in mission today is like a nation engaged in guerrilla warfare. There is no clearly defined battle line. . . . It is difficult, perhaps impossible, to design a grand strategy for mission. . . . The current educational scene is kaleidoscopic also. Who really knows what leads to commitment, or how men become moved to act? . . .

One thing seems clear. We need to be flexible in our approach. When there is no clearly evident right way, we should experiment with a variety of ways. . . . No denomination should be locked into a single approach. . . . We judge that the thematic approach to education is on the wane. Initiative for determining what people study and when they study it is shifting from the national to the local level. Fewer and fewer local congregations are willing to accept without question curriculum developed nationally. Adults, especially, are unwilling to study just because someone tells them they should. . . . It is extremely difficult . . . to convince all laymen everywhere that they should learn the same thing at the same time. . . . If the men of the First Church of Anytown suddenly become interested in the church and public education, why try to put off concern in order to study "Christ and the Faiths of Men" just because that is the theme for the year? Or if the women of the Second Church become vitally concerned about the ghetto, why shouldn't they set aside the mission theme for that year to launch an intensive study of poverty and race? Some Christian education boards are moving to encourage such initiative.

The mission planners were reading correctly the intention of many of the new curricula, as we have noted. The American Lutherans offered a four-track approach and challenged churches to choose. The United Presbyterians, the Episcopalians, and the United Church of Christ produced *Trends* magazine as a guide to local planning for study of varied resources. But it seems likely that the mission planners had a vision which went beyond many of the current denominationally structured efforts at flexibility. For the time being, at least, the pendulum may be swinging away from nationally planned curricula. How skillful the ordinary congregation might become in do-it-yourself designing is not at this writing quite so apparent.

Among the changing factors which will have to be taken into account by local churches and national planners as they design study for the future are the following.

New Methods and Media

Adults who stayed home from Sunday school to peruse *This Week,* the Sunday supplement of hundreds of newspapers, on February 13, 1966, could read sensational predictions of "a pill to make you more intelligent on days when you must take an important test, figure out a complex problem, or make a good impression, or a medicine, if you're a poor reader, that will help you become a good one by improving your ability to concentrate." "Soon you may be able to learn five times faster," readers were promised. Many teachers were probably eager to order the new pills immediately, both for their students and for themselves. Unfortunately, the article was not long on specifics or accounts of actual experiments, though it did say that a person's reading ability seemed to have been aided by dosages of acetamidobenzoate and that flatworms had actually been "taught" through injections.

Scientists offered the dream of "teaching medicines" but the reality of "teaching machines." In the 1960's the churches seemed little interested, but the public schools were beginning to find the new programmed instruction helpful indeed. In 1962 Association Press programmed Jack Finegan's little book *First Steps in Theology,* bringing it out under the title *Step by Step in Theology.* It is not known what reactions they got to this. It was to be noted, however, that, subsequently, neither they nor any other publishers flooded the market with programmed religious instruction materials.

The United Presbyterians experimented by programming two chapters of Suzanne de Dietrich's *The Witnessing Community.* Comparable groups were led in study of these chapters, some using the programmed and some the conventional materials. The Presbyterians found many objections to the programmed chapters. It is a slow, costly business to prepare the materials. (One rule of thumb is that it takes one hundred hours to prepare one hour of programmed instruction.) Adults are not used to this approach. Some resent it; others reject it for different reasons. There was only one argument for it, but it

was impressive. Those who had used the programmed
materials made almost double the test scores of those
using conventional books.

At Teachers College, Columbia University, where
he has been studying the new media, the Rev. A. O.
VanEck, Director of Adult Education for the Reformed Church in America, was asked about the
criticism that programmed instruction is based on a
behavioral psychology alien to the Christian faith.
"Not necessarily," he replied. "We may operate more
behavioristically than we want to admit. There may
be tension between the reinforcement theory and the
Christian view of man, but maybe we need to move
through this tension."

When a method has proved so successful in experiments and has become so useful in other education, it
seems inevitable that it will soon be used extensively
in the churches. No one proposes that programmed
instruction can replace the teacher or the cell group.
But for imparting information it does seem too good
to miss. The difficulty and high cost of production
make interdenominational development almost essential for the marketing of such materials.

"Unless you're willing to go all the way with TV,
forget it," Jack Fisler advised me. He spoke from
years of experience with the medium on the staff
of the Protestant Council of New York. "It is a big
and expensive business. But the Roman Catholics are
setting up their own TV network for their parochial
schools. They know the tremendous educational
opportunity it offers. Incidentally, one possibility
we've talked of here in New York is that the Catholics

might let the Protestants use their TV facilities during the Sunday school hour on Sunday mornings.

"There are big problems. One is expense. But the stations in New York have often been wonderfully cooperative. We've gotten a million and a half dollars worth of TV time with our annual $40,000 budget. There are all kinds of opportunities if we'd spend the money for them.

"The other problem is lack of coordination. The poor teacher now has either to throw out the curriculum or to ignore TV. If only there could be some planning so that the curriculum could help the teacher to use TV! The program "Davey and Goliath" for children has been a phenomenal success, with the whole series shown over and over Saturday mornings by New York stations. But generally Protestantism seems so short-sighted that we're missing the boat."

"TV tape recording offers many opportunities not provided by movies," VanEck added. His Reformed Church in America headquarters has begun extensive use of such equipment. "In a few years it may be common for churches to tape their own special programs or to show previously taped programs during their study hour."

In the electronic age it seems inevitable that Protestant educators will soon make more use of TV, both in programs they have produced and in discussion of commercially produced programs dealing with matters of serious concern. And only experts could keep up with the developments in 8mm sound and other electronic advances. "We are getting two or three inquiries a month for materials for overhead projectors," reported Thomas Nankervis of the Methodist Board of Education. Undoubtedly, the new media would influence the age-old message.

Games as aids to learning even for adults are likely to be a major development of the 70's. Already church groups are playing the Foreign Policy Association's "The Most Dangerous Game," imagining themselves diplomats forced to make decisions about war and peace. In Boston the National Council of Churches experimented with church participation in TV programs based on the game. By 1968 at least one denomination was experimenting with its own educational game program for men and women.

It seems likely to me that many churches will soon follow the pattern of St. Mark's Episcopal Church, Berkeley, California, or Madison Avenue Presbyterian Church, New York, in having a time for discussion after the service for those who wish to pursue further matters mentioned in the morning sermon.

But the perennial rediscovery of the power in letting small groups talk with each other personally about the Lord seems the surest predication of all. The most moving letter I received in correspondence with many churches described the experience of Pastor Paul B. Pierson of St. Luke's Lutheran Church, Bellevue, Washington. In his discussion groups, limited to eight members, people "discovered that they were not alone. People found each other and began bearing each other's burdens rather than calling on me. It was from these groups that for the first time people began to tell me that their lives were changing."

The Growth of General Adult Education

The final quarter of the twentieth century could offer not only new media but also new settings for religious education—the mushrooming adult education programs under secular auspices.

By the late 1960's there were already perhaps 25 million adults enrolled in study of one kind or another. Each student averaged some two enrollments, so that total registration in programs of adult education in the United States totaled approximately 50 million. A remarkable variety of institutions was sponsoring courses for adults. The YMCA, public high schools, colleges, and universities (including the various programs of the agricultural extension service) led the way in studies of subjects which were often of great relevance to the churches. But also such groups as the Ladies Garment Workers, business and professional associations, local libraries, and civic clubs were offering courses dealing with matters such as family life and civic concerns. Educational TV stations were multiplying across the nation. The *New York Times* predicted that between 1964 and 1974 one thousand new theaters and art centers would be built in the United States. Moreover, it was made clear by many surveys that the more secondary and university education one had, the more likely one was to participate in adult education programs. With universities expanding rapidly there was every reason, therefore, to predict a steady increase in continuing educational programs of many kinds.

It seems likely, and certainly desirable, that the churches will take note of this enormous enterprise and determine how best to relate themselves to it. As they seek to relate their message more closely to the world, the opportunity becomes all the greater.

Three kinds of relationships call for exploration:

1. Churches might well encourage their members to enroll in many existing programs. There is no need for churches to try to duplicate what is already being done as well under secular auspices. For example, evening colleges often offer courses in comparative religion, the problems of parenthood, and ethics. One can imagine churches planning programs designed to supplement from their distinctive perspective the offerings of local adult education centers.

2. Churches can solicit the cooperation of secular adult education agencies in setting up programs. For example, the Foreign Policy Association provides discussion materials which are authoritative, stimulating, and current and which are already being used in churches from St. Paul's Methodist in Tacoma, Washington, to First Baptist, Austin, Texas, as well as in the Congregational Church of Swampscott, Massachusetts. In Columbia, South Carolina, I heard a staff member of the local art museum describe to a group preparing to teach a course in church history how his institution stood ready to help them and their classes. Many churches are making use of professionals skilled in the area of human relations. But there are far more opportunities than are yet being used for the church

to profit from the services of adult education programs in their communities.

3. The church, in turn, needs to make its own resources for adult education more fully available to worthwhile community programs. For example, the notable community self-study conducted in the 1950's in the town of Falls Church, Virginia, and the one in the Twin Cities, described on pages 91-92, involved cooperation by the churches in a program under community-wide sponsorship. Churches in the San Antonio, Texas, area shared greatly in a program of basic adult education among Latin Americans there. But examples of this kind were still too few in the 1960's. If the church of the 70's is to take seriously its concern for mission in the world, such two-way cooperation in adult education needs to be expanded.

The Ecumenical Movement

One thing was clear about the simultaneous production of three *Mighty Acts of God* by three denominations and the publication of a host of similar books with slightly different titles. The needless duplication was a waste of the Lord's own money. I found no word in the Lutheran volume which would not have been acceptable to the Southern Presbyterians. The Canadian version seemed to describe essentially the same acts. It is interesting to speculate on what might have been done had Protestants combined forces in producing the millions of dollars' worth of curricula developed in the 1960's. Certainly the special needs of the inner city and of Appalachia could have been more fully considered, and programs of leadership training could have been strengthened.

There are signs that such wasteful duplication might be more and more avoided in the future. It may be seen from a study of the Appendix that most of the curricula of the 60's were produced jointly by two or more denominations. The trend seems likely to grow. The Consultation on Church Union offers the possibility of actual merger of at least some of these denominations. Indeed, it was rumored that one denomination had no program for revising their present materials. They felt that such major church unions would occur within so short a time that completely new approaches would be needed within eight years. Yet as late as 1968 educators of the denominations participating in the Consultation on Church Union rejected a proposal for a joint consultation on future adult curricula. Ecumenical production of study materials still has a long way to go, though it is clearly, if too slowly, on the way.

Vatican II brought what might prove a far more potentially revolutionary force into the picture. Already in the late 60's "living room dialogues" were taking place in communities all over the nation, bringing together Protestants and Catholics for the first joint discussions of theology that so many had shared since the Reformation. Often Jews, too, were part of the discussions.

It seems certain that such ecumenical contacts will grow. It is highly uncertain what will be their result. For some, they may bring a dulling of theological perception in an effort to express unity. For others, they may bring a sharpening of theological under-standing as points of view are compared and con-trasted.

It seems possible, at least, that the movement of Roman Catholic thought into Protestant discussions may serve as a balance against certain trends in the renewal movement. Catholicism has emphasized tradi-tion, has propagated what has seemed to Protestants an otherworldly kind of Christianity. Such an ap-proach might counteract the tendency of the renewal enthusiasts to preach a theology which, at its worst, seems to value novelty for its own sake and to dis-solve almost into pure humanism.

On the other hand, it is the liberal, renewal-minded Catholics who are most likely to enter into dialogue with Protestants. It may be that the two efforts at renewal will prove mutually reinforcing. The possi-bilities for good in adult education which might grow out of these contacts stagger the imagination. The danger, in my opinion, lies in Protestantism's too readily espousing a weak religion-in-general to make its needed contribution to the dialogue.

New Developments in Biblical and Theological Studies

"The emphasis on *The Mighty Acts of God* seems to be waning," comments C. Ellis Nelson. "One result is that the wisdom literature is being rediscovered." G. Ernest Wright had seemed almost of the opinion that Proverbs should not have been included in the canon. Such books as James Barr's *Old and New in*

Interpretation[2] have reminded the biblical theologians that there is much in Scripture which can be called revelatory which is not historical material. James D. Smart echoed this conclusion from a different approach when I asked him about trends. "We do not hear the Word simply by drawing inferences from historical events, as Wright suggests," he warned. While the curriculum books themselves recognized this, it is probably true that we are entering a phase of Bible study different from that which produced *The Mighty Acts* volumes.

"Suppose you left the seminary and went back to the Presbyterian Board of Christian Education in Philadelphia," I asked Dr. Smart, interviewing him in his office at Union Theological Seminary in New York. "What would you do now?"

"I'd continue to take just as seriously the importance of the central questions—thinking through theological concerns in Christian education," he replied. "Our biggest weakness in Christian education is that we have muffed this.

"Today the problem of tradition is central. This is the great neglected area. We act as though we could jump from the Bible to the world of today. It's a gap neither fundamentalists nor progressives know how to cross. The illusion of Presbyterians is that we have nothing to do with tradition. But we are part of a living continuum, one in which nothing ever stands still.

"Karl Barth knew this. He says frankly that his own work must now be done over again for a new generation. To think we can absolutize is the great error.

Each generation must work out its understanding of the gospel for its own day. In the Presbyterian Church I'd build on the Confession of 1967. In it we have spoken to the crisis of the church's existence today. Our real crisis is the threat of inhumanity, a strange ignorance of how to be human. The new Confession, therefore, focuses on reconciliation."

"How do you react to the notion that 'The world must write the agenda'?" I asked Dr. Smart.

"If that means that you don't enunciate a gospel in isolation from the actual world, it is true. There is no Word of God except as it comes to the world. It is futile just to tell Bible stories.

"But there are significant developments in theology which would start with man today and then seem to tailor the gospel to fit the mentality of that man. It is proposed that we won't talk about God any more since modern man doesn't understand that word. To that modern man I think the Scripture would reply, 'Good! Now with your idols gone maybe you will listen to what I have to say.' We need a dialogue between man and the Word. Man has a perfect right to put his questions to the Bible unconditionally. We must take critical scholarship seriously. But Scripture has its questions to put to modern man, too."

I got a somewhat less traditional answer from ecumenically minded William Jerry Boney, a young Presbyterian with a doctorate from Methodist-supported Drew Seminary, who teaches theology in a Baptist seminary in Richmond, Virginia, and maintains close ties with the Roman Catholics. Though thrilled by the prospect of ecumenical dialogue,

Boney sees the new theology as still largely fragmentary and incomplete. "Perhaps the day is past when individuals will produce whole systems of theology, as did Karl Barth," he suggested. "The religious education of tomorrow may be based on the work of teams of thinkers, Protestant and Catholic, with individuals attempting only partial answers to particular problems. Tomorrow's religious education may have to say frankly, too, that it simply can't answer a lot of questions, that it doesn't know a great many things, and yet that we can hold on to our faith in spite of our ignorance. We must learn to act even when we cannot yet fully answer."

The Renewal Movement and the Future of Adult Education

In one form or another discussion in any theological context of the future of adult education in Protestantism must deal directly with what we have called in this volume the "renewal movement."

It is obvious that this movement is not a single movement but many different and sometimes conflicting manifestations of a seeking for and finding of the Spirit. The Church of the Saviour has found its hope in part in a two-year course for new members. Some in Judson Memorial have at least discussed abandoning altogether the whole concept of church membership. The East Harlem Parish has emphasized new forms of worship. Christ Church, Burlington, Vermont, has abandoned weekly Sunday worship. East Harlem and Christ Church have emphasized task force involvement in action. Certain of the renewal centers have concentrated much more on intensive study of contemporary, or even radical, theology. No single approach predominates as a blueprint for the church of tomorrow.

Few, if any, of the centers of renewal claimed, however, that its own pattern represented *the* answer to the problems bedeviling the church. And within their diversity there was agreement on the necessity of new forms, new spirit, new action, and a new look at the new world.

If one looked for dangers in the renewal movement, these were not hard to find. "Of course church leaders today are theologically more sophisticated than those who preached the social gospel in the 1920s," Kendig Brubaker Cully commented to me, "but at least some of those who so strongly emphasize ministry or service in the world do seem to end up at just about the same place."

"If you want to read about 'education for mission' try the 1920 books of George Albert Coe," Robert Lynn tells his classes in Union Seminary, New York. It is hard to escape the feeling that the cycle has moved around to Coe again, and that a reaction to that approach will follow. If so, it seems safe to expect that sooner or later theologians will have to challenge the assumptions on which parts of the renewal movement do seem to rest. Sometimes, it appeared that by "evangelism" or "mission" some renewalists meant what in a former day would have been called simply the "social implications of the gospel." At times they appeared to be preaching what Paul would have condemned as a "salvation by works." Political action can never, of course, be the ultimate cure for the sickness in the individual heart. In the mid-60's the Avis Company adopted as its slogan "We try harder." There seems to be the danger that the far deeper message of the renewalists might degenerate for some into an effort to make the Christian church the Avis among service clubs, distinguished not because it had good news about Jesus, but because it tried harder to "serve" its fellow man. Probably all those named in this book realize this. George Webber has taught his students the need for piety, though of a new style. Elton Trueblood has emphasized the dependence of "fruits" on "roots." Gordon Cosby has spoken of the journey inward as well as the journey outward. Yet the tendency in the direction of simple activism does appear a danger.

In their very independence from established patterns and institutions the renewal experiments have encountered a double danger. On the one hand, many projects failed, split, or survived only in a weak form because of lack of organization, tradition, and financial support. On the other hand, some succeeded and ran in turn the danger of the institutionalization they had been created to attack. "This church is getting frighteningly successful," one member teased Howard Moody after a crowded service at Judson Memorial. "Even participation in a task force could degenerate into a new perverted piety," George Webber warns. "You go to church Sunday morning and work at the coffee house Tuesday night and think you have got right with God. At least this could become a danger."

It has been the case with some renewal movements in the past that in the second generation they have either disappeared or hardened into new orthodoxies. Let us pray that neither fate soon overtakes the current movement.

Sometimes its advocates' theology was heretical. Sometimes their denunciations were extreme. Sometimes their actual practice seemed disappointingly commonplace in spite of their brave ideals and florid publicity. But the worst thing about the prophets and programs of renewal has been that there weren't enough of them, for the church desperately needs to hear what they have to say.

Perhaps it emasculates their message to try to outline it. But here are four areas where the churches must heed the renewal prophets:

1. Adults must study the world in which they are called to witness. Perhaps it is Christ, not the world, who must set the agenda. The Scriptures must, of course, remain for Protestants the standard and norm. But Christian education is in no sense education nor truly biblical if it does not take seriously the twentieth century along with the first. It is people Christ came to save. And the people to whom today's church must witness are twentieth-century people. Their language is neither the Greek of the New Testament nor the Latin of church history. It is not the English of the British reformation. Nor is the world in which they are called to live for Christ the world of Palestine or the Roman Empire. We must study the world and ourselves in it or be ignorant of what it means fully to be Christian today.

2. Somehow the wedge must be removed between study and action. In its own way the Baraca-type Bible class knew this. Class activities sometimes obscured genuine study. The reaction, which sought to protect class time for study and to integrate the church's program which was so dangerously split among competing organizations, was needed. But too often group discussion never produced the action it discussed. The task forces and the vocational groups have found, not only a way to bridge the gap between study and action, but how to give a new quality of life to the study.

3. The new mission projects have reminded the church that it exists not for itself but for the world. Thus they have sought to call the attention of Christians to their need to witness to those who do not and perhaps never will go to church at all. It is a sad commentary on the state of the church that we are shocked by the thought of an educational project which seeks to befriend homosexuals. The average Bible class would hardly know how to begin to join the East Harlem Parish in a ministry to narcotics addicts. Even the atheists and agnostics who ask the very questions our classes are supposed to be able to answer seem outside our concern. The new endeavors have rediscovered whole segments of the population whose existence the traditional adult education programs had forgotten about or whom they had given up.

4. Perhaps the most important thing the diverse new endeavors share is a Spirit. This has been the greatest need of the Christian church. In itself, the music of a bearded guitarist is no more beautiful than

that of an organ. But the message of the new media is that something new is going on. God is not dead. Something is happening. In the various new institutes and churches one senses that people feel excited by the importance of what is happening. They are willing to try new things because they really believe that God will be at work in new ways. They may seem small and sometimes one-sided, and sometimes shallow. But their very faith made them whole. The new curricula were all well balanced. Pentecost, however, was not when men got a new balance but a new birth.

Renewal and the Role of the Educational Establishment

We have said that the ecclesiastical establishment, from denominational staffs to local church study planners, desperately needs to hear the message of even its bitterest opponents. For it seems to be entering the 70's in grave trouble. This is nowhere more evident than in its educational program. Denominational adult educators have made jokes about the announcements that God is dead—but they are aware that many churches really are dying. And the statistics on Sunday school enrollment, including adult enrollment, make such depressing reading that most with whom I talked avoided the figures altogether. The old forms clearly are reaching fewer and fewer of the new adults. Those who are attending Sunday school seem still too ignorant, and the whole church seems distressingly ingrown, concentrating on serving itself rather than the world.

Most educators look more hopefully toward the experiments than the experimenters realize. Thomas Wieser, who served as secretary of the revolutionary-minded North American Committee on the Structures of the Church, seemed surprised that I as a denominational educator wanted to interview him. "Most Christian educators seem to think we're somehow against them," he said. Perhaps that isn't quite true.

Indeed, as this book has tried to show, the line between the more radical renewal experiments and the denominational bureaucracies of the establishment is not as clear as it might seem. Many of the new programs are in the budgets of denominations. Usually even the most independent institutes seem glad to get gifts from suburban churches. And, on the other hand, it is when the denominational educators have taken most seriously the advent of a new culture—as notably in the Young Adult Project—that they have broken most completely out of established molds.

The inference, sometimes drawn from the new approaches, that the old structures are doomed seems exaggerated. In defense of the suburban church much needs to be said. It is *not* true that the establishment of numerous suburban churches represented *simply* flight. Churches were built in the suburbs because that is where most of the people are most of the time. Banks, supermarkets, department stores, all the things that make up a suburban shopping center have moved to the suburbs. They did this to reach people, not to escape from people. So did the church. In the suburbs the great majority of people live and a growing number work. Here, the majority of children and youth are educated. Indeed, a strong case can be made that the increasingly affluent society may look for its future pattern of life not to the slum but to the suburb. Perhaps men today have less and less of their lives invested where they work and more and more invested in other areas. To speak of the suburban captivity of the churches is to voice a truth. But to suggest that the suburban church cannot educate a man for the Christian life because of its geographic location is to go too far. Chapter IV suggested that there are ways in which suburban churches can transcend the values which their location in a complaisant and affluent culture seeks to impose upon them. The needed revival does not begin with sudden abandonment of all existing structures.

This is not the proposal of all those most interested in new structures. If my interest surprised Dr. Wieser his first proposal surprised me. "Begin where you are," he advised. Indeed, he even spoke of the remarkable opportunity of churches in my own conservative denomination located in the South.

Two attitudes toward the new experiments must be avoided by the denominational bureaucracies and the "successful" suburban churches. (1) We must not ignore what the prophets are saying. (2) We must not settle for a superficial hearing of it. A Madison Avenue campaign to make "ministry of the laity in the world" simply the "annual theme" will be a perversion of the rediscovered truth. And simply to multiply art festivals and feel that we have therefore come to grips with the world will, of course, not suffice.

Rather, we need to listen: to the experimenters,

including those who are most radically critical of the establishment, and to the world for which they seek to speak. The Anglican Church of Canada has set adult education a startling example. It is perhaps the first denomination in history to subsidize the writing of an attack upon itself. "There was absolutely hell to pay," admits staff member Colin Proudman. "That really 'put the cat among the pigeons'!" But the attack made the most repentance-provoking Lenten book in years. And regardless of the merits of the book (*The Comfortable Pew*[3]) , the notion of a church looking at itself as mirrored in the eyes of a disillusioned former member is challenging indeed. The prophets of renewal, by contrast, are, of course, not agnostics but committed Christians. They are, however, because of that very commitment, often disenchanted with the churches they see. Our Israel had better listen to these Amoses, critically indeed, but attentively. Most importantly, we must seek to hear behind their words the Spirit.

We ourselves, denominationally and in our local churches, need to experiment and to subsidize some of their experiments. The future is simply not clear enough for us to proceed except by trial and error. Businesses spend millions on research. The church has hardly begun to use the new research tools available. Perhaps the most hopeful pattern for denominational bureaucracies is that set by the Board of Church Extension of the Presbyterian Church, U. S. which announced in 1966 that it was making a quarter of a million dollars—a large sum for that small denomination—available for experimental projects. Local experimenters were encouraged to apply. The one stipulation was that no project would be considered which was in the established standard pattern. At least one Board of Christian Education is said to have made it a rule of thumb that if at least one third of their new projects did not fail, they simply weren't being creative enough.

One of the great truths which theologians such as Harvey Cox have been concerned to emphasize is this: God is at work not simply in the church but in the world. As congregations and denominations experiment in faith, they may make a corollary discovery. The Savior of the world is also still at work in his church.

Encounter with that Savior is adult Christian education.

APPENDIX

SOME OF THE
NEW CURRICULA

An exhaustive account of the new curricula of all the some 250 American denominations would fill several volumes. And these curricula themselves are constantly changing. If in Chapter III we have emphasized the similarity of the denominational efforts, in this Appendix we will point to some unique features of several of the more important ones.

The International Uniform Lessons

Before we look at the really new curricula, it is only fair to note that the old one showed some signs of new life. The curriculum which, in the early 60's, at least, still commanded the biggest and most loyal following was the International Uniform Lesson Series. The Baraca-type Bible class had been using the Uniform Lessons for decades. It planned to use them still. Every six years the Uniform Lessons had taken them on its circuitous, cyclic path through the Bible, with at least three months out of every year devoted to the study of Christ himself. American Protestantism owed no small debt to the Uniform Lessons, whatever their faults, for the fact that thousands of its members did indeed have more than a little familiarity with the Word.

Sales were actually up. From 1954 to 1964 the Uniform Lessons gained 8.9 percent in overall sales, with a 7.1 percent gain in adult materials. Annual circulation for adults was reported at 8,760,120. The National Council could advertise to newspapers the importance of carrying weekly commentaries on these lessons with the claim that "the odds are 17 to 1 that the Protestant church in your community uses the Uniform Lesson Series."

In some ways the old curriculum was adjusting to the new times. The quarterly temperance lesson was being ditched. In its place a whole series designed really to dig into the problem of temperance was scheduled for July–September, 1971. To answer repeated charges that the Uniform Lesson Series fragmented Scripture, the 1969-70 lessons included one year of straight-through-the-Bible survey. In a determined effort to keep up with the changing world the lesson series for October–December, 1972, called "The Bible Speaks to Issues of Our Time," is supposed to apply the Scriptures to such matters as revolution, modern science, totalitarianism, race relations, and world peace.

Better cooperation in publication was intended to improve the quality of the series. The Methodists, cutting back from five different treatments of the Uniform Lessons to one, were beginning each lesson not with an exegesis of scripture but with an account of a "persistent life need" to which that scripture seemed to speak. The United Presbyterians, the Southern Presbyterians, and the United Church of Christ were pooling resources for a single—presumably improved—edition.

"My hope," said Miss Muriel Walker, National Council staff member, "is that Uniform Lessons will be developed by the various denominations as a real depth Bible study. Actually, the ULS has been much maligned by a lot of people who haven't seen it for twenty years."

There were built-in problems with the Uniform Lessons, however—at least as many professionals saw them.

Inevitably, study seemed to focus on brief "printed" scripture passages, to neglect the context, and to fragment the Bible.

The lessons were forced by their structure to attempt the dangerous leap from Scripture to today, leaving no room for study of nineteen hundred years of intervening church history. In 1966 a new member of the committee which plans the Uniform Lessons proposed a series on church history, but he got nowhere.

Beginning with Scripture, the Uniform Lessons often failed to make contact with the man whose interests lay elsewhere, and too often in practice their study never led beyond the eighth century B.C.

The old materials had too long been associated with old ways of study. The denominational planners dreamed of new methods, more easily associated with new books.

The Cooperative Curriculum Project

One new curriculum venture can be expected to influence the religious education of 40 million Protestants for the next twenty years. The Cooperative Curriculum Project, under the auspices of the National Council of Churches, has good claim to being the most important religious education venture of this generation.

Beginning in December, 1960, the project involved 16 denominations, 125 denominational representatives, consultants in sociology, psychology, education, and theology, four years of effort, and seven week-long planning sessions, plus the work of many others in reviewing the manuscripts. The resulting city-telephone-directory-sized volume, *The Church's Educational Ministry: A Curriculum Plan,* broke down curriculum into five areas (life and its setting, revelation, sonship, vocation, and the church), 32 themes, and 108 "correlations." The key to the design was the concept of the intersection of concerns of the Christian faith with "basic persistent life issues." The plan offered a detailed and systematic proposal at every age level of the points at which the theological affirmations of the gospel most clearly intersect the recurring needs of man.

The result has been a foundation for Christian education impressive both psychologically and theologically. Major sections of the book relate the themes to adult life.

One is tempted to outline too simple an origin for the Cooperative Curriculum Project's major ideas. In the 40's and 50's Florence B. Stratemeyer of Teachers College, Columbia University, was advocating for public schools a curriculum which would relate the concerns of learners with society's needs and values. The key for understanding the intersection of these two she found in the concept of recurring "persistent life situations." [1]

At the same time, just across the street from Teachers College at Union Theological Seminary, theologian Paul Tillich was expounding his own idea of correlation between Christian doctrines and man's ultimate concerns.

Tillich's colleague Lewis J. Sherrill, professor of Christian education, now began to work out systematically his own correlation of psychological and theological concerns. In *The Gift of Power* (1955),[2] Dr. Sherrill published his conclusions. Thus mediated, Tillich's theology was filtered into the thinking of many Christian educators.

With this technique of correlation and intersection liberals and conservatives, theologians and psychologists could work together in harmony. There seemed to be something in it for everybody. Led in part by D. Campbell Wyckoff, professor of Christian education at Princeton Theological Seminary and a former student of Stratemeyer's whose own gospel-centered approach to curriculum was also clearly a factor, the Cooperative Curriculum Project planners were able to agree on a basic design.

When I proposed this oversimplified history to Muriel Walker, she smiled. "Stratemeyer was an influence on us, I'll agree. But she was only one among many influences. You can't get 125 people together from 16 different denominations and not have strong differences of opinion. The developmental psychology of Erik Erikson played an important part."

Dr. Wyckoff reminded me too of the influence on the group of Bernhard Anderson, with his emphasis on Scripture, and of Harold DeWolf's "neo-liberalism."

"Everyone who helped came with his own ideas," Miss Walker concluded. "The plan we came out with is frankly eclectic."

"Our goal," Dr. Wyckoff insisted, "has been to help local churches do their own planning, not to hand them a prefab structure." In 1967 Wyckoff was working closely with the Church of the Brethren as their staff members and seminary professors tried to develop plans, derived from the Cooperative Curriculum Project, for helping local committees select materials and patterns.

In balance, flexibility, completeness, psychology, and theology it seemed difficult to improve on the Cooperative Curriculum Project. At least one professor of adult Christian education remained somewhat skeptical, however. "It worries me that so many denominations could agree on it," he mused. "It threatens no one. It's too innocuous. There just isn't much controversial about it. Maybe that's its problem. Based on a concept of the self, it just isn't very prophetic."

There was, however, plenty of room in CCP-based curricula for controversial appeals for social justice. As the denominations enter the 70's, it remains to be seen how effective such appeals might prove to be. In the meantime there were plenty of competitors in the adult curriculum market.

American Baptists, Disciples of Christ, Church of the Brethren, Church of God (Anderson, Indiana), Baptist Federation of Canada

Five denominations are cooperating to produce a new curriculum based upon the Cooperative Curriculum Project. American Baptists and Disciples of Christ are in the process of joint publication. The Church of the Brethren and the Baptist Federation of Canada are also using this new graded series. The Church of God is publishing its own materials.

A key concept in the new plan is the idea of the *crossing point*. The term describes "the dynamic interaction between the gospel (the meanings, data, and experiences inherent in the gospel) and the concerns of the learner in his whole field of relationships." (Compare the ideas of "correlation" and "intersection" noted earlier.)

A three-year cycle centers around three perspectives: (1) knowing the Living God, (2) responding to God's call to live in Christ, and (3) being the community of Christian love. Materials for each six-month semester would include a student's book, a teacher's guide, a teaching kit of resources, and a magazine for each age group.

"This curriculum plan has three unique features," says Charles Oehrig, American Baptist adult editor: " (1) a thorough theological and educational structure, (2) a creative methodology designed to help groups move away from simply listening to lectures to an active involvement in the teaching-learning process, and (3) the annual perspective with a book of the year. This book provides a theological treatment of the annual perspective. Theologian Roger Hazelton has written the first of these, entitled *Knowing the Living God*. Ministers and qualified laymen can use this study in theological education of the laity, especially with church school teachers and parents. If a minister, taking his role as teacher of teachers seriously, uses a tool such as *Knowing the Living God,* he will become vitally related to the church's educational ministry."

The United Methodist Church

If the Cooperative Curriculum Project was the mother of the new Methodist materials, Marshall McLuhan, with his plea for a multimedia approach, was at least in part the father. Every teacher was expected to arrive in class armed with a packet which contained, for the first quarter of the Foundation Studies, poster-sized cartoons, modern paintings, wall-filling charts for evaluating group processes, large-print case studies and excerpts from contemporary drama, and a film clip showing mimes clad in tights and assuming poses which, the accompanying flexible record explained, illustrated "man's search for a meaningful faith."

Building on the Cooperative Curriculum Project's idea of the intersection of need and revelation, the series began with a course which attempted to relate Scripture to the logo-therapy of psychologist Viktor E. Frankl. Written by Robert C. Leslie, who had studied under Frankl, *Man's Search for a Meaningful Faith* followed a format departing radically from older patterns. There was no teacher's guide. Instead, every student was expected to use this same study book with the teacher, with group procedures suggested throughout the volume for all to join in. "We know this will threaten some teachers," Richard T. Murray of Perkins School of Theology admitted, "but we are serious about this idea of shared leadership." In addition to the study book each student was expected to own a companion volume of readings selected from such varied writers as Carl Rogers, Dietrich Bonhoeffer, and cartoonist Charles Schulz.

The United Presbyterians and the United Church of Christ

"No, the United Presbyterians are not abandoning Sunday school," staff member Ed Trefz laughed when I teased him about certain erroneous but widely circulated reports. "But

140

we are saying that not everybody has to study on Sunday morning. In fact, we're not going to launch a national program to get *everybody* to do anything."

The word "spectrum" seems to be the key to the new United Presbyterian and United Church of Christ approach to adults. "The Methodists have their basic books which everybody is expected to read," Trefz continued. "Our twelve Decade Books are comparable. But we're making no effort to prescribe these for everybody. Some of our folks are already above these books. Some need one but not the others. That kind of thing must be decided locally. Our job is to encourage a wide choice from a spectrum of materials and subject matter."

When I asked how the option would be provided, Mr. Trefz gave me a description of *Trends* magazine. While pilot issues of *Trends* concentrated on a single subject—the God-is-dead furor—the population explosion and various other controversial subjects have also been introduced. No session-by-session study suggestions are provided, but rather articles designed to stimulate and inform.

Rounding out the resources was a new journal, *Enquiry*, clearly seeking to carry on many of the features of the earlier journal *Crossroads*, with which Presbyterians had twenty years earlier pioneered in a distinguished way a new style of adult study quarterly.

The Presbyterians and the United Church of Christ had been laying especially heavy emphasis on leadership training and on creativity at the local level. Somewhere in the *Decade-Trends-Enquiry* resources, there should have been something for everybody, but the denominational staffs appeared quite sincere in their concern to help local churches create their own curricula out of any other materials that might suit their own situations better.

The Lutherans

We are fighting the "confirmation complex," says Donald Hoefferkamp of the Missouri Synod Lutherans. That is, the Lutheran tradition has been strong on confirmation classes for youth, but once these have been completed, the traditional Lutheran has tended to think his religious education complete.

Even so, traditional Lutherans, such as those of the Missouri Synod, were seeking to establish a new image. The first issue of *The Gate,* a new adult education periodical which they began to publish in the fall of 1967, contained detailed suggestions for a series of studies based on the modern novel *Lord of the Flies.* Plans called for studies of such contemporary literature to be a part of each issue.

Offering a three-track curriculum for adults, each issue of *The Gate* also included suggestions for three months of Bible study and three months of "skill study," dealing with such skills as prayer and witnessing.

Their cousins, the American Lutherans, used the confirmation tradition to help launch their new curriculum. They built the first materials for adults to coordinate with their youth confirmation materials, an extra bonus for the parents of youth being confirmed. PACE, however, left traditional Lutheran forms far behind.

Theirs was perhaps the only curriculum thus far to be worked out in cooperation with Hollywood. "For a while director of adult education Bob Konzelman was practically commuting to the film capital," a colleague laughed. "At first some of the movie people distrusted us—thought we were trying some new censorship scheme, perhaps. But Konzelman was able to convince them that our guides would mean more business for them. When one of the first films we reviewed turned out to be a surprise box office hit, they were impressed." Working against short deadlines, the Lutherans have been able to produce guides for the theological analysis of movies ready for use by the time the films hit the downtown theaters.

Lutheran adult educator Kenneth Alpers analyzed PACE for me around its four-track pattern:

1. The eight Challenge courses form a core which it is hoped that all Lutherans will study. The courses form a basic structure of knowledge, the kind of fundamental concepts Jerome Brunner talks about in secular education. Every Challenge student was expected to agree to attend all sessions and prepare weekly.

2. Encounter groups, limited to four couples each and bound by so set a discipline that they were not to meet without all present, studied such books as *The Present Tense of God,* by Halford Luccock, found their learning theory basis

more in the needs of individuals and in interpersonal relationships.

3. Insight classes were based on the tradition of the Uniform Lessons.

4. And Dialogue groups started with the modern situation, studied movies, as noted earlier, or perhaps studied contemporary social problems such as poverty, sex, and the church's role in society.

The Lutheran Church in America made its own movies, often of a highly professional quality. Their curriculum was introduced with a notable film, *Patterns of the Mind,* containing interviews with outstanding scientists. Subsequently, the "stimulus series" of films followed somewhat the same pattern. For example, one film showed Lutheran TV commentator Ray Sherer interviewing Lutheran statesman Orville Freeman about the role of the Christian in politics. Another film discussed Christianity and modern sculpture in an interview with Egon Weiner. Subsequently, however, the series may include dramatic stories as well as interviews.

There were books, too—a series of particularly attractive and readable paperbacks, beginning with the inevitable *Mighty Acts of God* and designed, usually, for one twenty-week course and two sixteen-week courses a year. Frank Klos, of the Lutheran staff, described for me also "school of religion" materials planned to supplement the church school books and designed for six- to ten-session exploration of such "worldly" concerns as abortion and Vietnam.

Materials in this "Impact" series included records, filmstrips, and other media along with the more conventional pieces.

The Episcopal Church

Among the major denominations the Episcopalians alone have successfully resisted the temptation to produce a new million-dollar curriculum for adults during the 1960's. "There are a world of good resources already available," explains Richard Johns. "We have concentrated more on helping adults to know how to use things all around them."

One step in this direction was the publication in 1967 of *A Book, a Group, and You,* a guide which would help a study group consider many different kinds of materials: religious books, novels, plays, and secular nonfiction. By 1968 they were also at work on a sequel, *An Issue, a Group, and You,* designed to help adults analyze theologically controversial events of the day. They also had an Episcopalian on the editorial board of *Trends,* the magazine designed to be a guide to resources for the local study of contemporary concerns.

The Episcopalians were producing some study packets, too, for short (six to eight weeks) study programs on such subjects as the relationship of law to grace—"Our people tend to come out on the legalistic side too often," says Richard Johns—and a packet on the Eucharist.

More typical of the Episcopalian trend, however, were the Church and Community Conferences in which little groups from several parishes might discuss the news in the morning paper and relate it to the good news of the gospel. Plans were developing for similar Church and World Conferences, in which the Episcopalians were hoping to make use of materials on foreign policy and peace for which tentative plans were begun in 1968 by a National Council of Churches' group. The Episcopalians have not abandoned their concern about small group work which had given rise to the notable parish life conferences of the late 50's and early 60's, but as the decade ends, they are putting a new emphasis on mission in the world beyond the group.

By 1967 the Episcopalians, the United Presbyterians, and the United Church of Christ had formed a long-range planning committee to study jointly the nature of the Christian education which would be needed in the 1970's and 80's.

The Southern Baptists

The biggest of the new curricula was in some ways the most conservative. The Southern Baptists, giant among Protestant Sunday schools in enrollment, launched their Life and Work curriculum in 1966 and soon had the majority of their adult students forsaking the Uniform Lessons for the new quarterlies.

Though the new materials were still very clearly Bible centered—they were probably closer to the Uniform Lesson tradition than any other of the curricula of the 60's—they did seek in new ways to deal with the contemporary needs of

Baptist adults. They were designed, too, to fit into a fivefold plan of Southern Baptist education, involving the highly effective Training Union, which still packed their church buildings on Sunday nights, and including other parts of their church life such as their elaborate system of choirs.

One distinguishing feature of the Southern Baptist approach is the unique emphasis on close grading—even of adults. Materials of their new curriculum are designated for younger adults, median adults, or older adults. Moreover, it is not uncommon to find classes segregated by sex and limited to a five-year age span: men 30-34, 35-39; women 45-49, etc.

"It's the secret of our growth," laughed one Baptist professor. "Walk into a Southern Baptist Sunday school building, and you can see how we emphasize small groups. The small adult classrooms are built so that when a group grows, it has to divide. We multiply by this kind of division, as more and more new little classes are formed."

The Presbyterian Church, U. S.; the Reformed Church in America; the Cumberland Presbyterians; the Associate Reformed Presbyterians; the Moravian Church.

An objective observer would probably call it the heaviest of the new curricula. Those involved in its production, as I am, would prefer to call it the most thorough. Either way, the Covenant Life Curriculum, with its 440-page annual books for students and 380-page annual books for teachers, provided professor-written volumes designed to lift the intellectual level of the Southern Presbyterians (and several other small denominations) in ways that might have gladdened and yet startled their father Calvin.

The volume-a-year pattern, continued through at least the first six years of the curriculum, was deliberately designed to push adults into deeper exploration. Moreover, while the Methodists claimed that their materials were comprehensible at about the ninth-grade level, and the United Presbyterians advertised that anyone who could understand the *Reader's Digest* could understand *Enquiry*, the Southern Presbyterians deliberately set their texts at the level of the high-school graduate. Theology, rather than psychology or the situation, was the chief factor in setting the design.

"We call our curriculum a 'spicle,'" Dr. Rachel Henderlite,

chief planner, used to say. "It is a spiral-cycle, repeating our three approaches to the faith (Bible, church, and life), but each three-year cycle builds systematically on the previous one."

Theologically the curriculum is rather conservative, reflecting considerably the influence of Karl Barth. But after the publication of *The Christian Life,* which was written for the Presbyterians by Methodist ethics professor Waldo Beach and which satirized suburbia and denounced traditional southern stands on race and labor, Bible-belt fundamentalists cried "heresy!" in spite of the book's Calvinistic dogma. This course was accompanied by posters with pictures such as a church bulletin board which advertised beneath a cross the invitation "Worship in air-conditioned comfort!" The church history materials included little records relating scenes from church history, such as a you-were-there glimpse of the Council of Nicaea. And even the Barthian-oriented year's study on doctrine invited students to listen to recorded excerpts from such plays as Tennessee Williams' *Suddenly Last Summer* and Archibald MacLeish's *J.B.* The Covenant Life Curriculum could boast not only depth but balance and a concern for communication.

SUGGESTIONS
FOR INDIVIDUAL OR
GROUP STUDY

If you are studying this book with other teachers or curriculum planners, here are some discussion questions or study suggestions to guide your group sessions.

Introduction

1. How many different forms of adult education are going on now in the churches of your community?
2. List the changes you can think of that have taken place in adult education in your church in the last ten years.
3. How do you personally react to the things going on in Protestant adult education? To what extent are they really preparing men and women to live as Christians in our day?
4. To get a fresh look at the new needs of Protestant adult education, view, if you can, the film *Patterns of the Mind,* used to introduce the new Lutheran curriculum. What new challenges to the church's educational program are presented by such new things as the development of life in the test tube and the invention of machines that think? (Order the film from almost any church film library.)

Chapter 1

1. How do you react to the quotation from Gordon Cosby on p. 18 that the church's "institutional structures that we know are not renewable"? What do you think of Cosby's

specific suggestions, such as possibly doing away with professional pastors and church buildings? What value could
such changes have?

2. In what ways, if any, do you think the church needs to be
   renewed?

3. Some adherents of the renewal movement would define
   the purpose of lay training as this: to equip church members to serve in the world. To what extent would you
   agree with this and similar ideas of Hendrik Kraemer,
   briefly summarized on p. 23? What, if anything, does this
   statement leave out?

4. Does your own church's educational program concentrate
   on things Christians do in church or things we do in the
   world? What kind of balance do you think there should
   be between these two areas of concern?

5. Which of the books of the renewal movement have you
   read? If you are studying *Cycles and Renewal* in a class
   now, could you report briefly on one of these at the next
   session?

6. Do you know anyone who could give your group a first-
   hand report on any of the independent movements mentioned in Chapter I or on any of the congregations it
   describes? A second-best approach would be to write some
   of the renewal programs for information to relay to the
   class. Here are some addresses:

   The Yokefellow Institute, 920 Earlham Drive, Richmond, Ind. 47374

   The Layman's Movement, Wainwright House, Milton
   Point, Rye, N. Y. 10580

   The Ecumenical Institute, 3444 Congress Parkway, Chicago, Ill. 60624

   The Christian Faith and Life Community, 2503 Rio
   Grande, Austin, Texas

   Faith at Work, 295 Madison Ave., New York, N. Y.
   10017

   The Detroit Industrial Mission, 8646 Puritan Ave.,
   Detroit, Mich. 48238

7. Can you tell the class from your own experience about a
   worship service comparable to those described on p. 35;
   a church theatrical production such as one might witness
   at Judson Memorial (pp. 35-36) ; a long program of train-

ing of new members, such as that of the Church of the Saviour (pp. 36-38) ?

8. What do you think of the idea of Christ Church, Presbyterian, Burlington, Vermont, which meets in an old TV repair shop, has no Sunday school or regular Sunday worship, but concentrates its efforts on little groups which serve in the world and whose study grows out of their service (pp. 38-40) ?

9. To get a vivid picture of the East Harlem Parish, view one of the following films: *We Hold These Truths, The Man on the 6:02, A Square Mile of Hope,* or the "Look Up and Live" TV presentation of the work of the parish, all available from the East Harlem Parish, 2050 Second Avenue, New York, N. Y. 10029.

10. To stimulate your thinking about Christ Church, Burlington, you might look at the film about it called *Burlington, Vermont,* a kinescope of a CBS television program in the "Look Up and Live" series in the group called "Beyond the Sanctuary." Available from Carousel Films and various denominational film libraries. 30 min., b/w.

Chapter 2

1. What were the adult classes like in the church in which you were a child? In what ways, if any, are they different in your church today? What values do you see in the different approaches?

2. With which of these gifts of the nineteenth century are you familiar today and what values have each: YMCA educational programs; summer conference centers; the International Uniform Lessons; big Bible classes for men or women?

3. To what extent does the adult education program in your church reflect the progressive ideals of Harry C. Munro (pp. 50-53) ; that is, is it varied, lively, relevant, lay-led, liberal, pointing toward service in the world?

4. To what extent does your adult program reflect the more conservative theology of the 40's and 50's?

5. What impression, if any, has group dynamics study (p. 57) had on the adult education program of your church?

6. At what points, if any, in its history does it seem to you

that Protestant adult education has progressed? At what points did it take a wrong turn?

Chapter 3

1. Obviously, the best way to study this chapter is to look at the materials of the new denominational curricula and compare them. If your class is made up of people from only one denomination, each class member should borrow material from friends in other churches and bring it to the study. What can you learn from what the others are doing that will help you in your own church?
2. If your class is made up of people from different denominations, each member should bring samples of his own curriculum to show the others. Each should be prepared to describe in a few minutes the best things about his new curriculum.
3. An entertaining session could center around seeing and hearing some of the new audio-visual materials that form so important a part of most new curricula.
4. Does the description in the Appendix of this book of your church's new curriculum seem fair? What are the most important things it fails to say?
5. Probably some in your class are not using a denominational curriculum. What seem to be the advantages and disadvantages of their approach?

Chapter 4

1. This chapter suggests that many churches have experimented with exciting new approaches to adult education. It might make an interesting session for you and others in your class to report to each other the most interesting new things your churches have tried in adult education in recent years.
2. Chapter IV lists several ways in which churches have tried to relate their study to the world of the late twentieth century. Which of the following has your congregation tried, and with what results?
    Serious study of ethical issues—pp. 87-89
    Attacking community problems—pp. 89-92
    An accent on the arts—pp. 92-95

Task and mission groups—pp. 95-96
Vocational groups—pp. 97-99
Partnership projects—pp. 99-100
Special programs in family education—pp. 100-102
Older adult projects—pp. 103-4
Special younger adult ministries—pp. 104-7

3. Which of the above may be especially needed in your church or community? What value might there be for your church, alone or with others, to set up programs of these kinds?

4. An interesting session could center around an experiment in study related to one of the arts. For example, you might plan a theological analysis of a worthwhile film or television program. You might invite someone from the local art museum to suggest to the class how his institution might help in your study programs.

5. If there are those in your churches who have done some unusually interesting study experiments, they might be invited to report at one class session on what they have done.

Chapter 5

1. In the light of this chapter and this book, what do you predict education for adults will be like in your church fifteen years from now?

2. With which of the trends described in this book are you most in sympathy? Which, if any, seem dangerous?

3. What sort of education might the churches of your community offer jointly rather than separately?

4. How well prepared is your church to take advantage of the new technical developments in education, such as video tape and 8mm sound film?

5. What opportunities for adult education are offered in your community by state universities, community colleges, or evening classes in high school? To what extent could the churches of the area make use of these opportunities in the future? (You might want to ask someone involved in public adult education in your area to meet with your class to discuss this with you.)

6. As you think about future adult education in your own church, what do you think it ought to try to do? What

should be its goal? What kind of balance should it attempt between serving the adults of your church and preparing them to serve others? What sort of balance should it have between study of the Bible and study of the world today? What should be the place of the study of history and doctrine and the study of contemporary problems like war and poverty and race prejudice? What is the proper relationship between study and action?

7. In short, in the light of this study, plan what you would like to have studied and the way you would like to have it studied in your church for the next few years.

NOTES

Introduction

1. David Dempsey, "The End of 'Black Book' Publishing," *Saturday Review,* October 14, 1967, p. 27.

1. The Renewal Movement

1. John R. Fry, "The Denominational Dollar," in *Who's Killing the Church,* Stephen C. Rose, ed. (Chicago: The Chicago City Missionary Society, 1966), p. 66.
2. Gordon Cosby, "Not Renewal, But Reformation," in *Who's Killing the Church,* p. 53.
3. Howard Moody, "Toward a Religionless Church for a Secular World," in *Who's Killing the Church.*
4. Henri Godin and Yvan Daniel, "France a Missionary Land," in *France Pagan?* Maisie Ward, trans. (New York: Sheed and Ward, 1949), pp. 63-191.
5. D. T. Niles, *That They May Have Life* (New York: Harper, 1951).
6. Tom Allen, *The Face of My Parish* (London: SCM Press, 1954).
7. Hendrik Kraemer, *A Theology of the Laity* (Philadelphia: Westminster Press, 1959).
8. Peter Berger, *The Noise of Solemn Assemblies* (Garden City: Doubleday, 1961).
9. Gibson Winter, *The Suburban Captivity of the Churches* (Garden City: Doubleday, 1961).
10. Harvey Cox, *The Secular City* (New York: Macmillan, 1965).
11. *The Church for Others* (Geneva: The World Council of Churches, 1967).

12. Lee Gable, *Church and World Encounter* (Philadelphia: United Church Press, 1964).

13. Donald G. Bloesch, *Centers of Christian Renewal* (Philadelphia: United Church Press, 1964).

14. Robert Raines, *New Life in the Church* (New York: Harper, 1961).

15. George W. Webber, *God's Colony in Man's World* (Nashville: Abingdon Press, 1960).

16. Webber, *The Congregation in Mission* (Nashville: Abingdon Press, 1964).

17. Elizabeth O'Connor, *Call to Commitment* (New York: Harper, 1963).

18. Bruce Reinhart, *The Institutional Nature of Adult Christian Education* (Philadelphia: Westminster Press, 1962).

19. John R. Fry, *A Hard Look at Adult Christian Education* (Philadelphia: Westminster Press, 1961).

20. Letty Russell, *Christian Education in Mission* (Philadelphia: Westminster Press, 1967).

21. D. Elton Trueblood, *The Company of the Committed* (New York: Harper, 1961).

22. For more on the philosophy of the Yokefellow movement see *ibid.*

23. For more on the East Harlem Parish see the works of Webber and Russell cited in notes 15, 16, and 20 above.

24. For more on Judson Memorial see the article by Moody cited in note 3.

25. O'Connor, *Call to Commitment*, p. 27. For more on the Church of the Saviour, see this book and her more recent *Journey Inward—Journey Outward* (New York: Harper, 1968).

26. Quoted from "A Proposal," a mimeographed document dated June 6, 1966, and distributed to the members of Christ Church. The quotation appears in the appendix to *The Church for Others* (see note 11 above), p. 129.

2. Some Cycles in the History of Lay Education

1. James T. Carey, *Forms and Forces in University Adult Education* (Chicago: Center for the Study of Liberal Education for Adults, 1961) pp. 16-17. The quotation is attributed to Paul Voelker, "The University of Chautauqua," NUEA Proceedings (Madison, Wis., 1915), pp. 241-42.

2. Kendig Brubaker Cully, *The Search for a Christian Education Since 1940* (Philadelphia: Westminster Press, 1965), p. 38.

3. Kenneth Stokes, "Major Trends in Cooperative Protestant Adult Education, 1936-64" (University of Chicago Dissertation, 1965). To this important work I am much indebted in this chapter.

4. Richard E. Lentz, *Making the Adult Class Vital* (St. Louis: Bethany Press, 1954).

5. Zeigler was dean of the Presbyterian College of Christian Education in 1931 when he wrote *Toward Understanding Adults*. Later he left the professorship for a position with the Board of Christian Education of the United Presbyterian Church. Sherrill, professor of Christian education at Louisville Theological Seminary, later at Union, New York, teamed with J. Edwin Purcell of the Presbyterian U. S. (Southern) Board in 1936 to write *Adult Education in the Church*. Both books thus illustrate the close association of school and denominational administration.

6. See especially Sara Little, *The Role of the Bible in Contemporary Christian Education* (Richmond: John Knox Press, 1961) and Cully, *The Search for a Christian Education Since 1940.*

7. Harrison S. Elliott, *Can Religious Education Be Christian?* (New York: Macmillan, 1940).

8. H. Shelton Smith, *Faith and Nurture* (New York: Scribner's, 1941).

9. After leaving the Presbyterian Board, Dr. Smart published *The Teaching Ministry of the Church* (Philadelphia: Westminster Press, 1954), a book which was to be widely influential in spreading his views. Dr. Smart later became a professor of Bible at Union Theological Seminary in New York.

10. See, for example, the widely read *The Church Redemptive,* by Howard Grimes (Nashville: Abingdon Press, 1958).

11. Carl R. Rogers, *Client-Centered Therapy* (Boston: Houghton Mifflin, 1951), especially chap. IX.

12. Sara Little, *Learning Together in the Christian Fellowship* (Richmond: John Knox Press, 1956).

13. Robert S. Clemmons, *Dynamics of Christian Adult Education* (Nashville: Abingdon Press, 1958).

14. Paul E. Bergevin and John McKinley, *Design for Adult Education in the Church* (New York: Seabury Press, 1958).
15. Reuel Howe, *The Creative Years* (New York: Seabury Press, 1959).
16. Paul Maves, *Understanding Ourselves as Adults* (Nashville: Abingdon Press, 1959).
17. John Casteel, *Spiritual Renewal Through Personal Groups* (New York: Association Press, 1957).
18. Robert E. Koenig, *The Use of the Bible with Adults* (Philadelphia: Christian Education Press, 1959).
19. Helen Khoobyar, *Facing Adult Problems in Christian Education* (Philadelphia: Westminster Press, 1963).
20. David J. Ernsberger, *A Philosophy of Adult Christian Education* (Philadelphia: Westminster Press, 1959).
21. Lawrence C. Little, ed., *The Future Course of Christian Adult Education* (Pittsburgh: University of Pittsburgh Press, 1958).
22. Lawrence C. Little edited papers and addresses of this conference also, under the title, *Wider Horizons in Christian Adult Education* (Pittsburgh: University of Pittsburgh Press, 1962).

3. The New Curricula

1. Lawrence C. Little, *A Layman's Appraisal of Christian Adult Education* (Pittsburgh: Department of Religious Education, University of Pittsburgh, 1964), pp. 71-72.
2. As reported in the *Presbyterian Outlook,* November 14, 1966, p. 3.
3. "A Study of Religion in American Life" (Nashville: The Methodist Publishing House, Central Research, unpublished material, 1966).
4. *United Presbyterian National Educational Survey,* Lauris B. Whitman, Barey J. Keating, and Robert W. Matthews, eds. (Philadelphia: The Board of Christian Education, 1966).
5. The three *Mighty Acts* are by Arnold B. Rhodes (Richmond: John Knox Press), John B. Hardie (Toronto: The United Church Publishing House), and Robert J. Marshall (Philadelphia: Fortress Press), all 1964.
6. *The Church's Educational Ministry: A Curriculum Plan*

(St. Louis: Bethany Press for the Cooperative Curriculum Project, 1965) , p. 40.

7. Karl H. Hertz, *Teachers' Guide for Christian Behavior* (Philadelphia: Lutheran Church Press, 1964) , p. 7.

8. *The Church's Educational Ministry: A Curriculum Plan*, p. 8.

9. Among the relevant research is David R. Hunter's 1952 Ed.D. dissertation at Harvard on *Leadership and Group Productivity*. Dr. Hunter carefully compared the learning of adults in ten church classes taught by the same teachers using "group-centered" methods involving more free discussion and planning by the participants. His conclusion: "In this short-term course there is no dramatic difference between the two methods of leadership in terms of subject matter returns." Students in the leader-centered classes actually seemed to learn more facts. However, quite important for the church, "group-centered methods are highly preferable in terms of behavior change and the development of a cohesive group structure." In all ten group-centered classes the students did actually do some of the things proposed in the course, while in only one of the leader-centered classes was there significant change. And the group-centered class members developed friendships far more than the others. (See the abstract of this research in *Religious Education*, XLVIII [1953], 180.)

Richard J. Hill's notable study showed little difference between the results of discussion groups and lecture groups either in facts learned or in resulting activities. It is to be noted, however, that the lecture groups were led by university professors and other experts in the subjects studied, while the discussion groups with which he compared them were in the hands of relatively untrained leaders. This seems to suggest that the church is wise to use the discussion method in courses which are to be taught by those who are not authorities in the subject matter being studied. Again Hill's study indicated that more friendships were formed in the discussion groups, a matter of significance to the church. (See *A Comparative Study of Lecture and Discussion Methods* [The Fund for Adult Education, 1960].)

For a summary of many research projects comparing lecture and discussion, see the article by W. J. McKeachie: "Research on Teaching at the College and University Level," in *Handbook of Research on Teaching*, N. L. Gage, ed. (Chicago: Rand McNally, 1963), pp. 1118 ff. McKeachie notes that many experiments have seemed inconclusive but concludes that at least for changes of attitudes small group discussion is probably to be preferred.

10. Hertz, *Teachers' Guide for Christian Behavior*, p. 6.
11. Byron L. Johnson, *Need Is Our Neighbor* (New York: Friendship Press, 1966).
12. Jack E. Weller, *Yesterday's People* (Lexington: University of Kentucky Press, 1965).
13. Marshall McLuhan, *Understanding Media* (New York: McGraw-Hill, 1964), Chap. 1.

4. Creativity in the Congregation

1. Charles E. Mowry and Earl R. Williford, *Directions for a Young Adult Ministry* (Nashville: Division of the Local Church, General Board of Education of The Methodist Church, 1965), p. xi.
2. Charles E. Mowry, "Champion in the Urban Arena," *Christian Advocate*, January 13, 1966.

5. Some Predictions and Proposals

1. Paul R. Mort, *Educational Adaptability* (New York: Metropolitan School Study Council, 1953), pp. 2-5.
2. James Barr, *Old and New in Interpretation* (New York: Harper, 1966).
3. Pierre Berton, *The Comfortable Pew: A Critical Look at Christianity and the Religious Establishment in the New Age* (Philadelphia: Lippincott, 1965).

Appendix: Some of the New Curricula

1. Florence B. Stratemeyer, Hamden L. Forknew, Margaret G. McKim, A. Harry Passow, *Developing a Curriculum*

for Modern Living (2nd ed.; New York: Bureau of Publications, Teachers College, Columbia University, 1957), p. 117.

2. Lewis J. Sherrill, *The Gift of Power* (New York: Macmillan, 1955).